P9-BIQ-730

Math in Focus

Singapore Math®
by Marshall Cavendish

Extra Practice

Author

Hwa-Heng Heng

Marshall Cavendish
Education

U.S. Distributor

Houghton
Mifflin
Harcourt

COMMON
CORE

© 2013 Marshall Cavendish International (Singapore) Private Limited
© 2014 Marshall Cavendish Education Pte Ltd
(Formerly known as Marshall Cavendish International (Singapore)
Private Limited)

Published by Marshall Cavendish Education
Times Centre, 1 New Industrial Road, Singapore 536196
Customer Service Hotline: (65) 6213 9444
US Office Tel: (1-914) 332 8888 | Fax: (1-914) 332 8882
E-mail: tmesales@mceducation.com
Website: www.mceducation.com

Distributed by
Houghton Mifflin Harcourt
222 Berkeley Street
Boston, MA 02116
Tel: 617-351-5000
Website: www.hmheducation.com/mathinfocus

Cover: © Mike Hill/Getty Images

First published 2013

Math in Focus® Extra Practice Course 3B
ISBN 978-0-547-57900-9

Printed in Singapore

6 7 8   1401   17 16 15 14
4500499004   B C D E

Contents

Math in Focus
Singapore Math®
by Marshall Cavendish

Introducing Math in Focus® Extra Practice

Extra Practice was written to complement **Math in Focus®: Singapore Math® by Marshall Cavendish**. It offers further practice for on-level students and is very similar to the Practice exercises in the Student Books.

Practice to Reinforce and Challenge

Extra Practice provides ample questions to reinforce all concepts taught, and includes challenging questions in the Brain@Work pages. These challenging questions provide extra nonroutine problem-solving opportunities, strengthening abstract reasoning powers that include the use of mathematical structures, repeated patterns, models, and tools.

Using the Cumulative Practice

Extra Practice also provides Cumulative Practices that allow students to consolidate learning from several chapters. They can be used to prepare for Benchmark Tests or as another source of good problems for class discussion.

Using the Extra Practice

Extra Practice is an excellent option for homework, or it may be used in class or after school. It is intended for students who simply need more practice to become confident, secure mathematics students who are aiming for excellence.

 Extra Practice is also available online and on the Teacher One Stop.

CHAPTER

7 The Pythagorean Theorem

Lesson 7.1   Understanding the Pythagorean Theorem and Plane Figures

For each figure, shade two right triangles and label the hypotenuse of each triangle with an arrow.

1.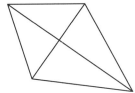

2.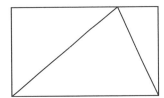

Find the value of x.

3.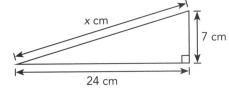

4.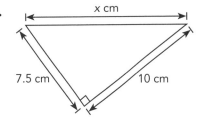

5.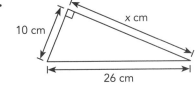

6.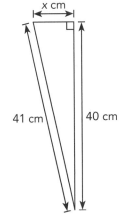

Name: _____   Date: _____

Calculate each unknown side length. Round your answer to the nearest tenth.

7.

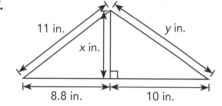

11 in.   y in.   x in.   8.8 in.   10 in.

8.

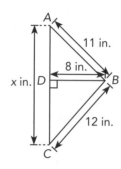

A   11 in.   8 in.   x in. D   B   12 in.   C

9.

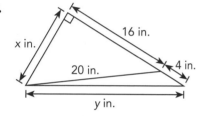

x in.   16 in.   20 in.   4 in.   y in.

10.

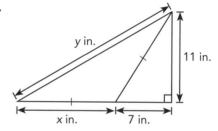

y in.   11 in.   x in.   7 in.

Solve. Show your work. Round your answer to the nearest tenth.

11. Fritz mows two triangular fields. Determine which field is a right triangle.

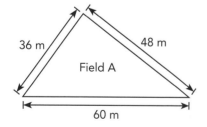

36 m   48 m   Field A   60 m

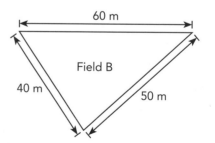

60 m   Field B   40 m   50 m

Solve. Show your work. Round your answer to the nearest tenth.

12. Alan placed a ladder against a wall. The bottom of the ladder was 5 feet away from the wall. Find the height of the wall.

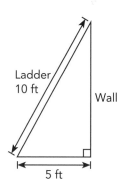

Ladder 10 ft

Wall

5 ft

13. One end of a cable is attached to the top of a flagpole and the other end is attached 6 feet away from the base of the pole. If the height of the flagpole is 12 feet, find the length of the cable.

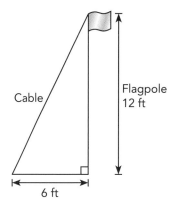

Cable

Flagpole 12 ft

6 ft

14. An escalator runs from the first floor of a shopping mall to the second floor. The length of the escalator is 30 feet and the distance between the floors is 12 feet. Find the distance from the base of the escalator to the point on the first floor directly below the top of the escalator.

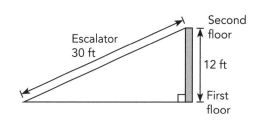

Escalator 30 ft

Second floor

12 ft

First floor

Name: _____   Date: _____

Solve. Show your work. Round your answer to the nearest tenth.

15. A hot air balloon is attached to the ground by a taut 100-meter cable, as shown in the diagram. Find the vertical height of the balloon above the ground.

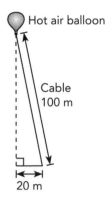

Hot air balloon

Cable
100 m

20 m

16. A taut cable connects two cable car stations A and B which are positioned 50 meters and 20 meters above the ground. The horizontal distance between the stations is $\frac{1}{2}$ kilometer. Find the length of the cable.

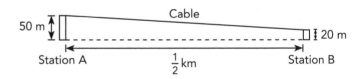

Cable

50 m

20 m

Station A

$\frac{1}{2}$ km

Station B

17. A whiteboard is 6 feet long and 3 feet wide. Find the length of the longest straight line that can be drawn on the whiteboard.

Solve. Show your work. Round your answer to the nearest tenth.

18. Sono Road runs from South to North and Ewest Road runs from East to West intersecting at point *X*. Jeb and Jill are at point *P* on Sono Road 30 meters from point *X*. Jeb walks along Sono Road to point *X* then turns east and walks 20 meters to point *Q* on Ewest Road. Jill walks on a path linking point *P* to point *Q*. Find the difference in distance between the two routes.

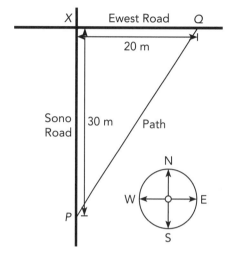

19. A 15-foot vertical pole has two strings of equal length attached to it at different points. The other end of one string, represented by $\overline{AB}$ in the diagram is tethered to the ground 12 feet from the base of the pole. The other end of the other string, represented by $\overline{CD}$ in the diagram is tethered to the ground 13 feet from the base of the pole.

a) Find the length of the string.

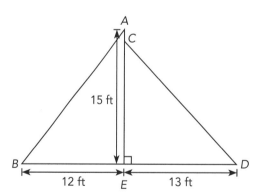

b) Find the distance between the points *A* and *C*.

Name: _____   Date: _____

Solve. Show your work. Round your answer to the nearest tenth.

20. The diagonal of a square piece of cardboard is 28 inches.

    a) Find the perimeter of the square.

    b) Find the area of the square.

21. In the diagram, m∠ADB is 90°, AD is 22.6 inches, BC is 13 inches, and AB is 34.4 inches.

    a) Find the length of $\overline{AC}$.

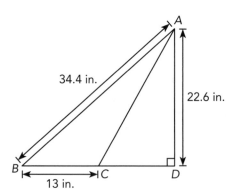

    b) Find the area of triangle ACD.

Name: _____   Date: _____

Solve. Show your work. Round your answer to the nearest tenth.

22. Points *A*, *B*, and *C* are corners of a triangular field where m∠*ABC* is 90°, *AB* is 40 meters and *BC* is 45 meters.

    a)   Find the length of $\overline{AC}$.

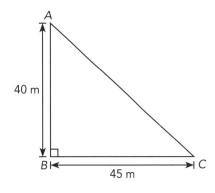

    b)   John walks along the edge of the field from point *A* to point *C*. If *P* is the point on $\overline{AC}$ when John is nearest to point *B*, find the length of $\overline{BP}$.

23. In rectangle *PQRT*, *PQ* is 80 feet, *QR* is 65 feet, *RS* is 30 feet, and m∠*SUP* is 90°.

    a)   Find the perimeter of the shaded triangle.

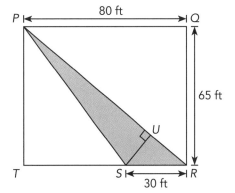

    b)   Find the area of the shaded triangle.

    c)   Find the length of $\overline{SU}$.

Name: _____   Date: _____

Solve. Show your work. Round your answer to the nearest tenth.

24. A map with a scale of 1 : 50,000 shows the locations of four towns A, B, C, and D. The distance between Town A and Town B is 6 centimeters, the distance between Town B and Town C is 7 centimeters, and the distance between Town C and Town D is 8 centimeters. Given that m∠ABC = m∠ADC = 90°, find the actual distance between Town A and Town D.

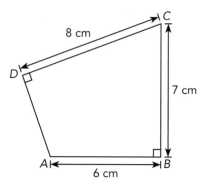

25. In the diagram, *AB* is 20 meters, *BC* is 65 meters, *CD* is 60 meters, *AD* is 16 meters, and *BD* is 25 meters. Determine if triangle *ABD* and triangle *BDC* are right triangles. Explain.

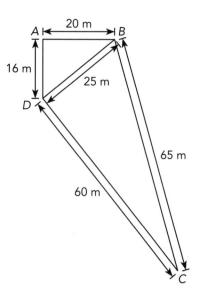

Lesson 7.2   Understanding the Distance Formula

Solve. Show your work. Round your answers to the nearest tenth if necessary.

1. Points $P(-4, 3)$ and $Q(4, -3)$ are plotted on a coordinate plane. Find the exact distance between points P and Q.

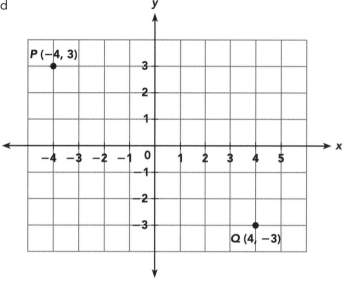

2. Find the distance between each pair of points. Which pair of points are the least distance apart?

   a) $A(3, -2)$, $B(0, -4)$

   c) $E(3, -3)$, $F(-7, 8)$

   b) $C(4, 2)$, $D(2, -6)$

   d) $G(-1, -4)$, $H(-2, -5)$

3. Samantha plots the points $P(-3, 4)$, $Q(3, 3)$, and $R(4, -3)$ on a coordinate plane. She joins the three points to form triangle PQR. Is the triangle a right triangle? Explain.

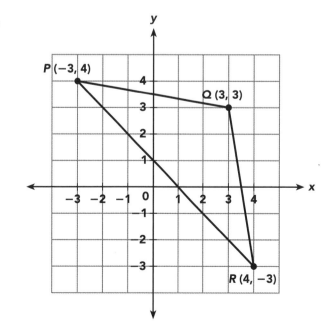

Name: _____   Date: _____

Use the data in the diagram for questions 4 to 6. Each unit on the grid equals 1 kilometer.

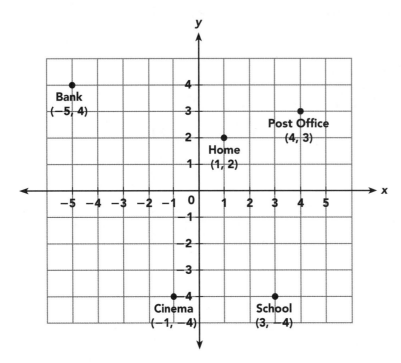

4. Find the approximate distance from Mary's home to each of the following locations.

   a) Bank   **b)** Cinema   **c)** Post Office   **d)** School

5. Which three locations are the same distance from Mary's home?

6. On a particular day, Mary traveled from her home to school. After school, she went to the post office to mail a letter. Then, she went home. Find the total distance she traveled.

Solve. Show your work.

7. Town A and Town B are located at the points shown in the diagram. Mr. Appleton wants to drive from Town A to Town B. He can choose between the route that takes him through Towns P and Q, or the route that takes him through Town R. Each unit on the grid equals 1 kilometer.

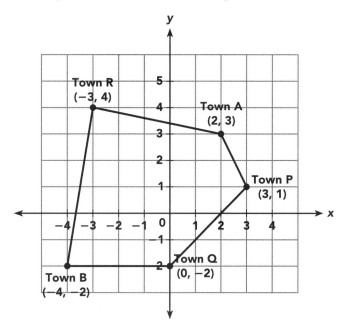

a) Which is the shorter route?

b) What is the difference in distances of the two routes?

Name: _____   Date: _____

Solve. Show your work. Round your answer to the nearest tenth.

8. The positions of a boat and a lighthouse are shown on the grids. Each unit
    on the grid equals $\frac{1}{2}$ mile.

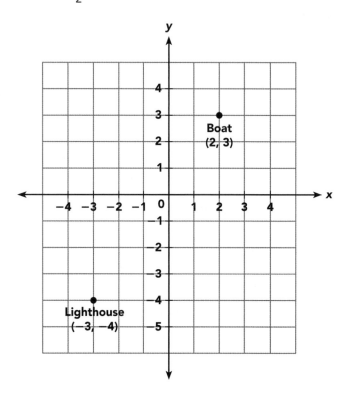

a) How far is the boat from the lighthouse?

b) The boat takes 20 minutes to travel to the lighthouse. Find the speed
    of the boat in miles per hour.

Name: _____ Date: _____

Lesson 7.3   Understanding the Pythagorean Theorem and Solids

For this practice, you may use a calculator. Use 3.14 as an approximation for π.
Round your answer to the nearest tenth when you can.

For each solid, find the value of the variable.

1.

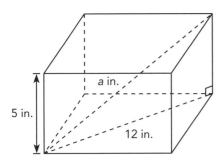

5 in.   *a* in.   12 in.

2.

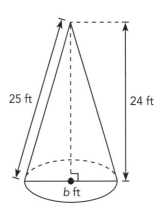

25 ft   24 ft   *b* ft

3.

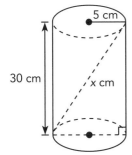

30 cm   5 cm   *x* cm

4.

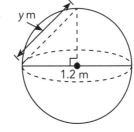

y m   1.2 m

Name: _____   Date: _____

Solve. Show your work. Round your answer to the nearest tenth.

5. Fred bought a paperweight in the shape of a square pyramid, as
    shown in the diagram. Find the total surface area of the paperweight.

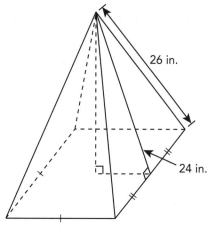

26 in.

24 in.

6. Helen made a conical lampshade out of a piece of cardboard. She wants to
    paint the surface of the lampshade. Find the surface area of the lampshade,
    given the dimensions in the diagram.

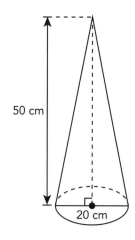

50 cm

20 cm

7. A cone was placed inside a cylindrical container. The cone and the container
    have the same base, 50 inches, and the same height, 40 inches. Find the
    slant height of the cone.

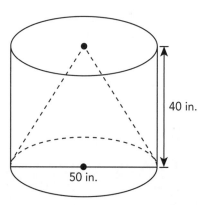

40 in.

50 in.

Solve. Show your work. Round your answer to the nearest tenth.

8. A rectangular box measures 30 centimeters long,
    20 centimeters wide, and 15 centimeters high, as
    indicated by the diagram. A spider sits at point A
    while a fly lands at point N. Point N is the midpoint
    of $\overline{HG}$. To catch the fly, the spider crawls from point A
    to point M, a point directly below the fly, before
    climbing up to the fly.

    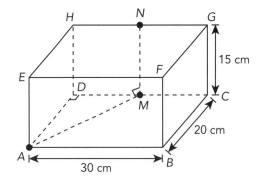

    a) Find the distance from point A to point M.

    b) Find the shortest distance between the fly's initial position and the
        spider's initial position.

9. A composite solid is made up of a cone and a cylinder. The diameter of the
    cylinder is 3 feet and the slant height of the cone is 3 feet. The cone and the
    cylinder have the same height. Find the height of the composite solid.

    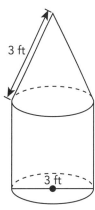

Solve. Show your work. Round your answer to the nearest tenth.

10. Figure A shows a conical paper cup with a height of 9 inches and a slant height of 10 inches. The cup is cut along a slant edge. Figure B shows the cup spread open on a flat surface. Find the perimeter of Figure B.

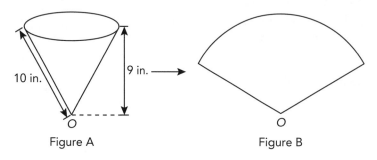

Figure A   Figure B

11. The diagram shows a square pyramid with height 4.5 meters. The length of each slant edge is 5 meters.

a) Find the length of a diagonal of the base.

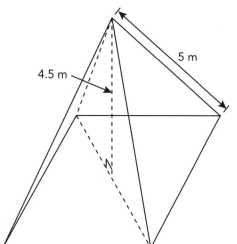

b) Find the area of the base of the pyramid.

Name: _____   Date: _____

Lesson 7.4   Identifying Volumes of Composite Solids

For this practice, you may use a calculator. Use 3.14 as an approximation for π.
Round your answer to the nearest tenth if necessary.

1. Find the volume of each of the following composite solids.

a) A cylinder that sits on top of a triangular prism

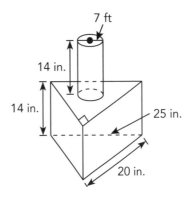

b) A cone that sits on top of a cylinder

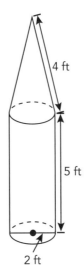

2. A cylinder has a hemispherical hole cut from the top of it. The shaded rim is 3 inches thick. Find the volume of the solid.

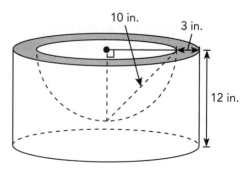

10 in.

3 in.

12 in.

3. The diagram shows a composite solid made up of a hemisphere on top of a cone.

a) Find the height of the cone.

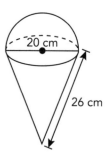

20 cm

26 cm

b) Find the total volume of the solid.

4. Joanne made a jewelry box in the shape of a rectangular prism with the shape of a square pyramid.

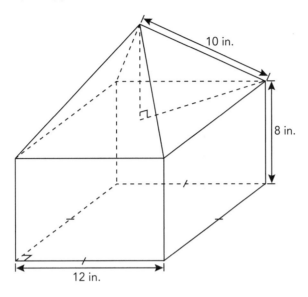

a) Find the length of a diagonal of the base of the jewelry box.

b) Find the height of the cover.

c) Find the total volume of the jewelry box.

5. A metallic cylinder has a cone-shaped hole cut out of it, as shown.

a) Find the depth of the hole.

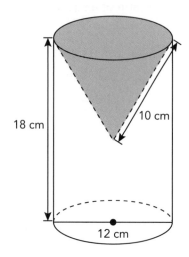

b) Find the volume of the remaining metal.

6. Miley is decorating the Young Writer's Corner in her class. She makes a large model of a pencil by using a cylindrical piece of wood and a cone at one end for the tip. She uses a hemispherical piece of foam for the eraser at the other end of the pencil.

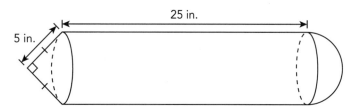

a) Find the radius of the eraser.

b) Find the volume of the entire model of the pencil.

7. A sculpture is made out of a triangular prism with a pyramid extending out from one of its sides. The sculptor made the length of all the edges of the solid 10 inches.

a) Find the height of the pyramid.

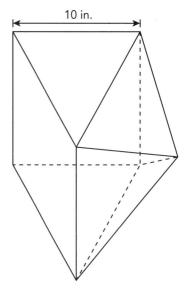

10 in.

b) Find the volume of the solid.

8. Raven ordered a new wooden nameplate for her office desk. The nameplate is made of a triangular prism attached to a 0.6 inch high base. The base is in the shape of a rectangular prism. Find the volume of the entire wooden nameplate.

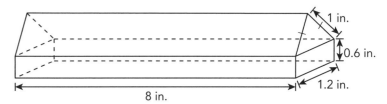

1 in.

0.6 in.

1.2 in.

8 in.

CHAPTER

7 **Brain @ Work**

1. Gavin plots the points C (4, 2), P (8, −10), Q (6, 8), R (−8, 6), and S (−8, −2). Using point C as the center of a circle, he draws a circle such that the circumference of the circle passes through three of the other points.

   a) Determine which point does NOT lie on the circumference of the circle. Explain.

   b) Does the point in **a)** lie inside or outside the circle? Explain.

2. Carl builds a model of a rocket using two cylinders of equal height, and a cone. He cuts the cone into two parts, one for the middle and the other for the tip of the rocket. The heights of the two cylinders are equal. Find the approximate surface area of the model. Use 3.14 as an approximation for π. Round your answer to the nearest square inch.

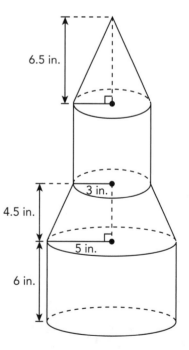

6.5 in.

3 in.

4.5 in.

5 in.

6 in.

Name: _____ Date: _____

CHAPTER

8 Geometric Transformations

Lesson 8.1   Translations

Find the coordinates of the image under each translation.

1. A (−2, 5) is translated by 7 units to the right.

2. B (3, −7) is translated by 2 units to the left and 8 units down.

3. C (8, −4) is translated by 6 units to the right and 7 units up.

Draw the image under each translation.

4. $\overline{DE}$ is translated 3 units to the left and 4 units up.

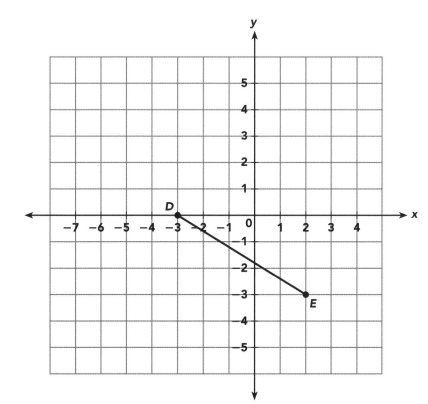

Draw the image under each translation.

5. Triangle *FGH* is translated 4 units to the right and 3 units down.

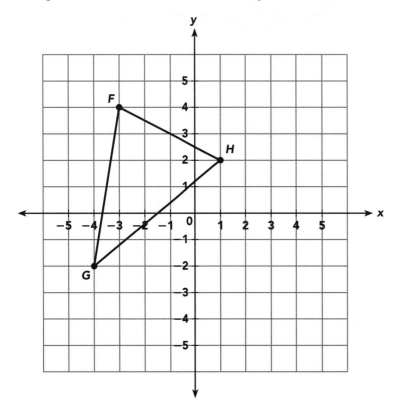

Find the coordinates of each point using the given translation. Label the images on the coordinate plane.

6. Alan's home is located at *H* (−3, 4). He uses the translations described in
   a) to **d)** to walk his dog.

   a) From *H* (−3, 4), translate by 2 units to the left, 3 units up to *P*.

   b) From *P*, translate by 6 units to the right, 2 units down to *Q*.

   c) From *Q*, translate by 1 unit to the right, 8 units down to *R*.

   d) From *R*, translate by 11 units to the left, 5 units up to *S*.

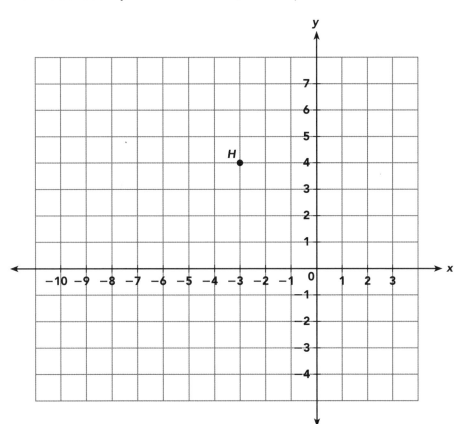

Name: _____   Date: _____

Solve. Show your work.

7. A piece of plastic with vertices *A* (3, 2), *B* (2, 4), *C* (−1, 1) and *D* (4, −3) is
moved by a translation to a new position *A′B′C′D′*. If the coordinates of *A′* are
(6, −1), find the coordinates of the images of *B′*, *C′* and *D′*. Draw *A′B′C′D′* on
the coordinate plane.

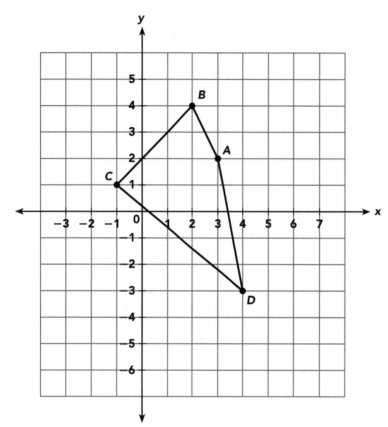

Name: _____   Date: _____

Solve. Show your work.

8. An object on the floor of a warehouse has a triangular base. Peter moved the
    object from its position at *ABC* under a translation that moves each point
    (*x*, *y*) to (*x* + 3, *y* − 2). Given *A*(−2, 3), *B*(2, 4), and *C*(7, −1), find the coordinates
    of *A'*, *B'*, and *C'*. Draw *ABC* and *A'B'C'* on the coordinate plane.

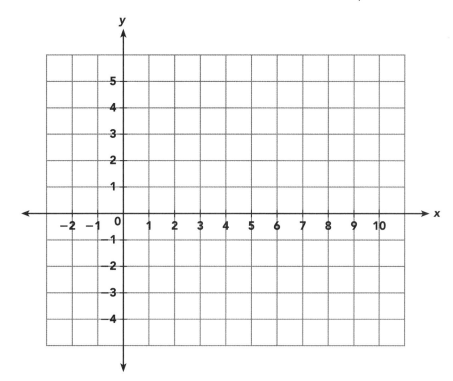

Solve. Show your work.

9. A computer program T guides a robot to move an object on the coordinate plane 5 units to the left and 3 units up. $\overline{AB}$ is translated by T to $\overline{A'B'}$. What are the coordinates of A and B given $A'(7, 3)$ and $B'(2, 1)$?

10. A line has the equation $y = x - 3$. It is translated by 2 units to the right and 7 units down. What is the equation of the new line? How do the slopes of the line and its image compare?

11. On a coordinate plane, an object at $P\,(-2, 3)$ is copied by moving it to the point $P'(5, -1)$. Describe the translation of this point both verbally and algebraically.

Lesson 8.2 Reflections

Draw and label the image using the given reflection.

1. Reflection in the x-axis

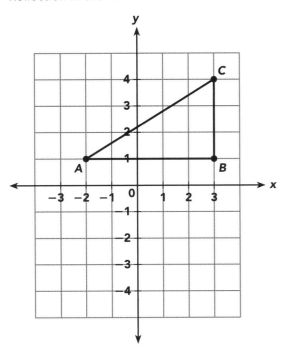

2. Reflection in the y-axis

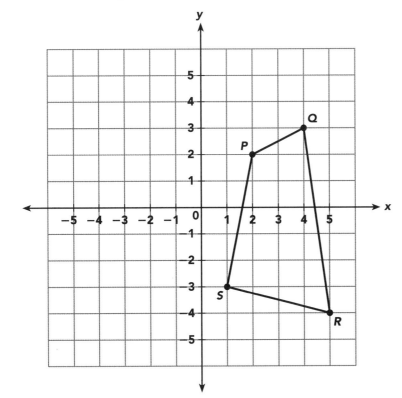

Draw the image using the given reflection.

3. The positions of two sticks $\overline{AC}$ and $\overline{BD}$ are shown in the coordinate plane. Draw the images $\overline{A'C'}$ and $\overline{B'D'}$ with $y = 1$ as the line of reflection.

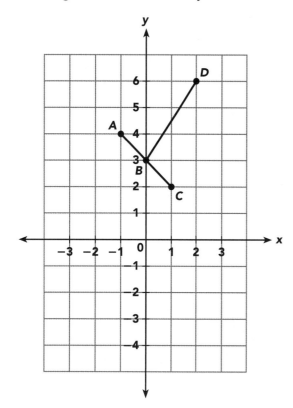

Solve. Show your work.

4. Figure *ABCD* is drawn in the coordinate plane. It is repeated by first reflecting it in the *y*-axis to obtain the figure *A'B'C'D'*. The image is further repeated by reflecting it in the *x*-axis to obtain the figure *A"B"C"D"*.

   Complete the table by finding the position of each of the other images.

Locations	Reflection in the y-axis	Reflection in the x-axis
A (−1, 3)	A'(,)	A"(,)
B (−3, 1)	B'(,)	B"(,)
C (−6, 1)	C'(,)	C"(,)
D (−6, 4)	D'(,)	D"(,)

   Then, draw and label figure *ABCD* and the respective images on the coordinate plane.

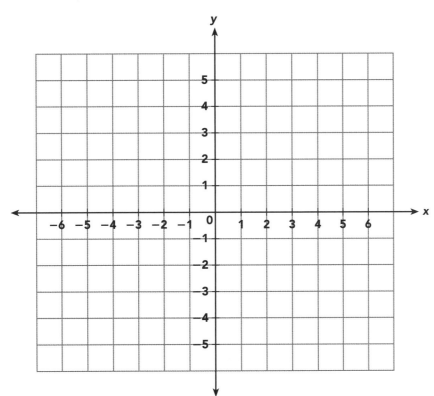

Solve. Show your work.

5. A graphic designer is drawing a logo in a coordinate plane. Some of the points
    are at A (−1, 5), B (−1, 3), C (−3, 1) and D (1, 1).

    a) Draw the line x = 2 on the same coordinate plane.

    b) The designer reflects the logo in the line x = 2. What are the coordinates
        of A', B', C' and D'? Draw A'B'C'D' on the same coordinate plane.

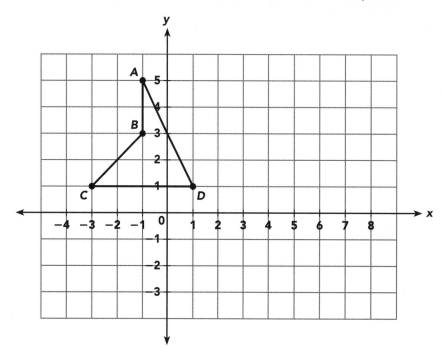

Solve. Show your work.

6. A symmetrical object, *ABCD*, is drawn in the coordinate plane. Three vertices of the object are at positions *A* (−3, 3), *B* (3, −3) and *C* (3, −5).

a) Draw and label points *A*, *B* and *C*.

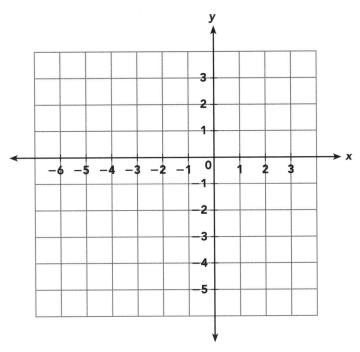

b) Point *B* is the reflection of point *A* in the line of symmetry. Find the equation of the line of symmetry.

c) Find the coordinates of point *D*. Draw *ABCD* on the same coordinate plane given above.

7. A kite has vertices *ABCD* with $\overline{BD}$ as its main diagonal. The positions of two of the vertices are *A* (2, 4) and *C* (−3, 1).

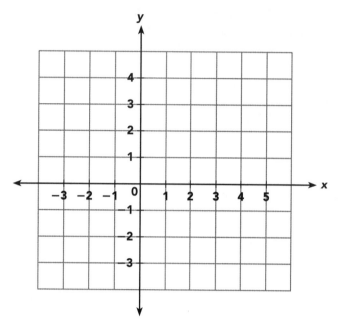

a) Draw and label *A* and *C* in the coordinate plane.

b) Find the equation of the main diagonal.

c) A point *P* lies on the kite. It has coordinates *P*(−4, −1). Find the coordinates of its image *Q* after a reflection in the diagonal $\overline{BD}$.

Solve. Show your work.

8. A figure *PQRS* in a coordinate plane is symmetrical about the line $y = 1 - x$.
The vertex *Q* is the reflection of *P* in the line $y = 1 - x$.

  a) If the coordinates of *P* are $(-4, 1)$, draw and label point *Q*.

  b) If the coordinates of *S* are $(-3, -4)$, find the coordinates of *R*.

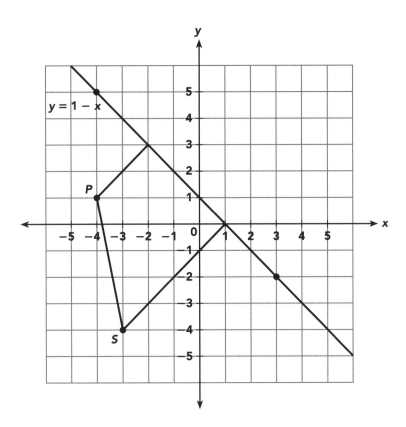

  c) Describe the figure *PQRS*.

Lesson 8.3 Rotations

Solve. Show your work.

1. A rotation of point *P* in the direction indicated about *O* maps *P* onto *P'*.
   State the angle of rotation.

   a)   Counterclockwise   **b)**   Clockwise

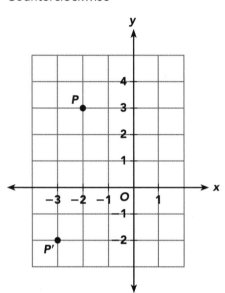
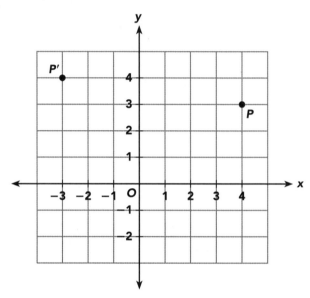

2. Each point has been rotated about the origin, *O* to form its image. State the angle and
   the direction of each rotation.

   a)   **b)**

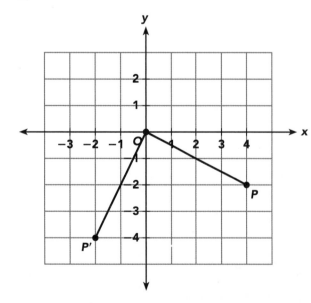
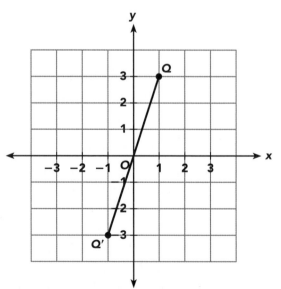

Solve. Show your work.

3. Peter is in the seat of a Ferris wheel rotating about its center *O*. The seat is at a point *P*. He is rotated from *P* by each of the following rotations. Draw and label his positions after each rotation from *P* on the coordinate grid.

   a) *A*: clockwise rotation of 180°

   b) *B*: clockwise rotation of 270°

   c) *C*: counterclockwise rotation of 90°

   d) *D*: counterclockwise rotation of 45°

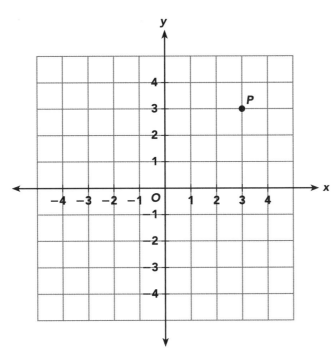

Solve. Show your work.

4. A spinner rotates about the center, *O* of a circular board. Initially, the spinner is in the position represented by $\overline{OP}$.

    a) If the spinner rotates to the position represented by *OA*, describe the rotation.

    b) A point *B* (−3, 2) undergoes the same rotation. Find the coordinates of its image *B′*.

    c) A point *C* also undergoes the same rotation. Its image is *C′* (−1, −3). Find the coordinates of *C*.

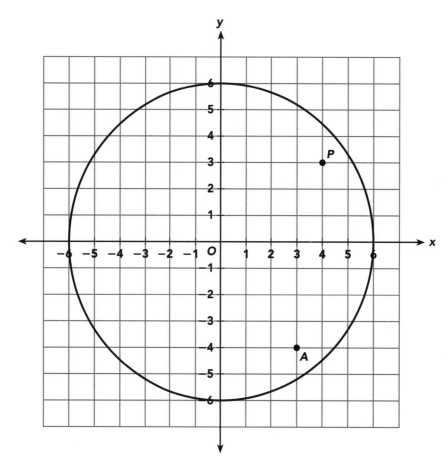

Solve. Show your work.

5. The diagram shows the minute hand of a clock rotating about the center, O of the clock face. The minute hand is initially represented by $\overline{OP}$. Point P is at position (3, −4). Find the position of the minute hand under each of the following rotations.

   a) Image P′: rotation of 90° counterclockwise

   b) Image P″: rotation of 90° clockwise

   c) Image P‴: rotation of 180° counterclockwise

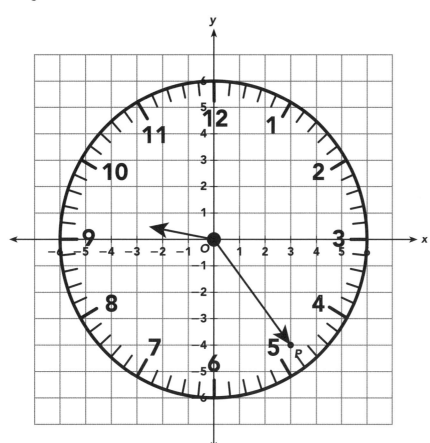

Name: _____   Date: _____

Solve. Show your work.

6. A trapezoid, *ABCD*, is drawn on the coordinate plane.

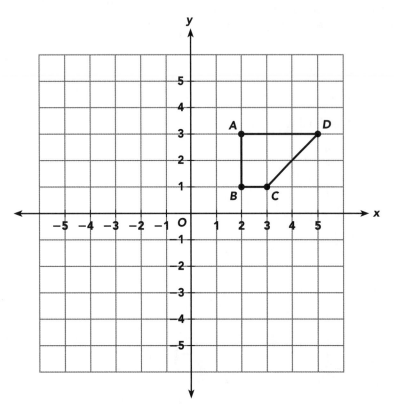

a) *ABCD* is rotated 90° counterclockwise about the origin *O*. Draw and label the image of *A'B'C'D'*.

b) What are the coordinates of *A'*, *B'*, *C'*, and *D'*?

c) *ABCD* is rotated 180° clockwise about the origin, *O*. Draw and label the image of *A"B"C"D"*.

d) Find the coordinates of *A"*, *B"*, *C"*, and *D"*.

e) How are *A'B'C'D'* and *A"B"C"D"* related?

Solve. Show your work.

7. A regular pentagon *ABCDE* is rotated about its center *O*, so that
   its appearance stays the same, but the vertices are rotated to
   different positions. The pentagon is rotated so that the vertex
   A moves to the original position of *B*. Describe two possible
   rotations, stating each angle of rotation and the direction.

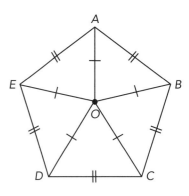

8. $\overline{P'Q'}$ is the image of $\overline{PQ}$ under a rotation about *O*. Explain, without using a
   coordinate grid, how you would obtain the position of *O* by construction. Show
   your construction clearly.

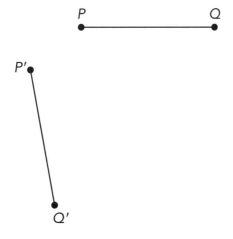

Lesson 8.4   Dilations

Tell whether each transformation is a dilation. Explain.

1.

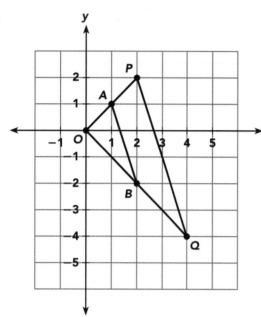

2.

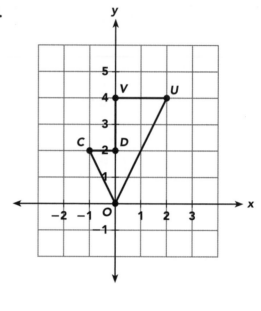

Solve. Show your work.

3. Susan has a triangle with side lengths of 3 inches, 4 inches, and 5 inches on a computer screen. She uses the computer to make some dilated copies of the triangle. Find the length of the sides of each copy with the scale factor given in **a)** to **d)**. In each case, state whether each copy is an enlargement or reduction of the original triangle.

   a)   Scale factor: 3

   b)   Scale factor: $\frac{1}{2}$

   c)   Scale factor: 1.2

   d)   Scale factor: 80%

Complete on the coordinate grid.

4. Each figure is mapped onto its image by a dilation with its center at the origin, O. Draw each image.

   a) Scale factor 1.5

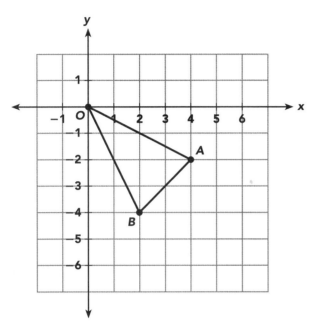

   b) Scale factor −1

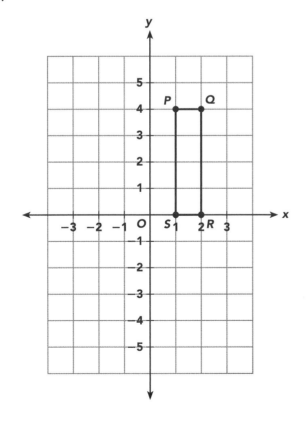

Name: _____   Date: _____

Complete on the coordinate grid.

5. Each figure is mapped onto its image by a dilation with its center at the origin, O.
Draw each image.

a) Scale factor $-\dfrac{1}{2}$

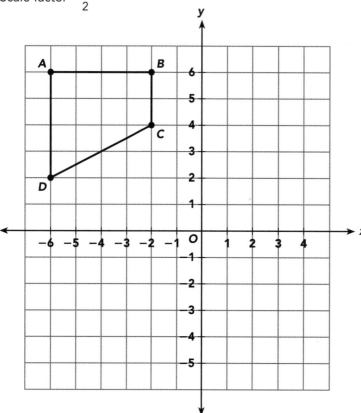

b) Scale factor 2

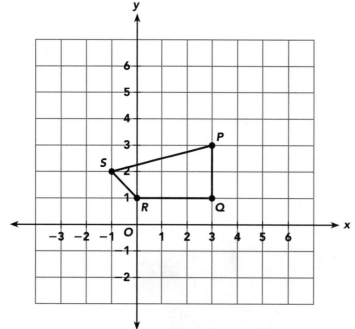

Solve. Show your work.

6. Points *P* and *Q* are mapped to their images by a dilation with its center at the origin, *O*.

   a) If the position of *P* is at (−3, 2) and its image is at (−9, 6), find the scale factor.

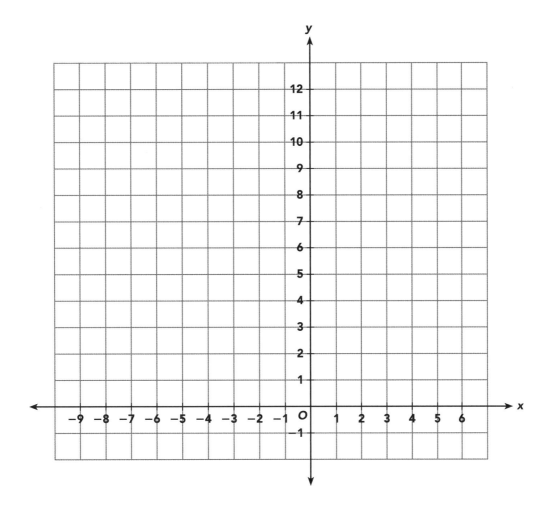

   b) If the image of *Q* is positioned at (3, 12), find the coordinates of *Q*.

Solve. Show your work.

7. A circle, with radius 1 unit and center at C (2, 3) is dilated to obtain a circle with radius 3 units and center at C' (5, 4).

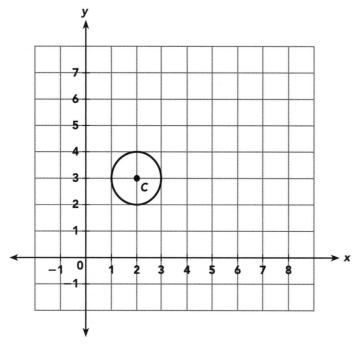

a) Find the scale factor.

b) Determine the center of dilation.

Name: _____   Date: _____

Solve. Show your work.

10. Triangle *ABC*, positioned at *A*(1, 1), *B*(2, 1) and *C*(2, 4), is mapped by a dilation of scale factor 2 about the origin, *O*, to obtain the image of triangle *A'B'C'*.

   a)   Mark and label the positions of triangle *ABC* and triangle *A'B'C'* on the coordinate plane.

   b)   Another dilation of scale factor −2 about the origin, *O*, maps triangle *ABC* onto triangle *A"B"C"*. Mark and label the position of triangle *A"B"C"*.

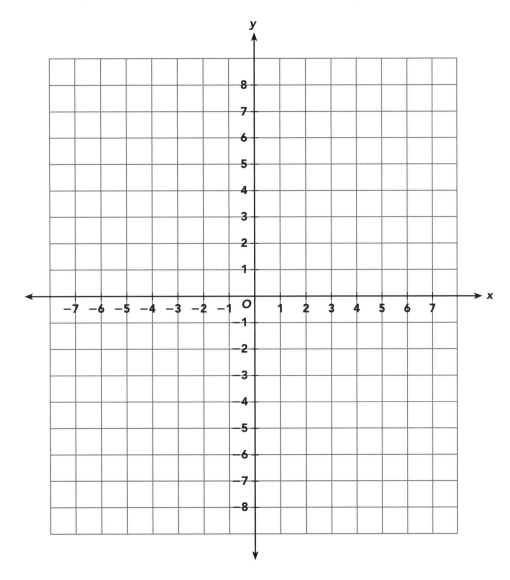

   c)   Triangle *A'B'C'* can be mapped onto triangle *A"B"C"* by a single transformation in two ways. Describe each of the two ways.

Lesson 8.5 Comparing Transformations

Complete.

1. A triangle with coordinates *A* (3, 1), *B* (4, 0), and *C* (5, 3) is drawn on the coordinate plane. Four other triangles are images of triangle *ABC* after each of the transformations in **a)** to **d)**.

   a) △*ABC* is mapped onto △*DEF* by a translation of 6 units to the left.
   Draw △*DEF*.

   b) △*ABC* is mapped onto △*GHI* by a reflection about the x-axis.
   Draw △*GHI*.

   c) △*ABC* is mapped onto △*JKL* by a rotation of 180° about the origin, *O*.
   Draw △*JKL*.

   d) △*ABC* is mapped onto △*PQR* by a dilation with center, *O*, and scale factor 2.
   Draw △*PQR*.

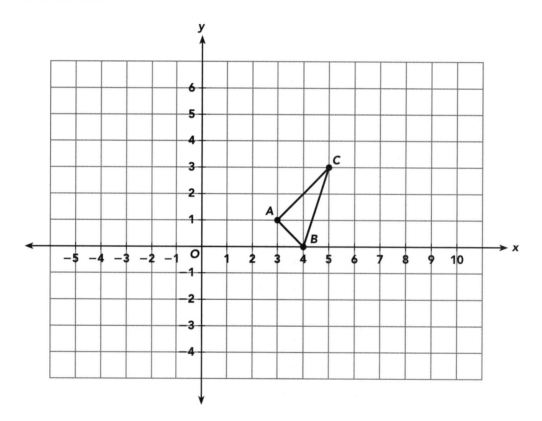

   e) Which of the transformations result in images which are exactly the same shape and size as △*ABC*?

   f) Which of the transformations results in images that have the same shape as △*ABC* but are of different sizes?

Solve. Show your work.

2. Quadrilateral *PQRS* with coordinates *P* (−1, 4), *Q* (−6, 3), *R* (−6, 1), and *S* (−3, 1) undergoes the following transformations.

   a) *PQRS* is mapped onto *P'Q'R'S'* by a reflection about the *y*-axis. Draw *P'Q'R'S'*.

   b) *PQRS* is mapped onto *P"Q"R"S"* by a reflection about the *x*-axis. Draw *P"Q"R"S"*.

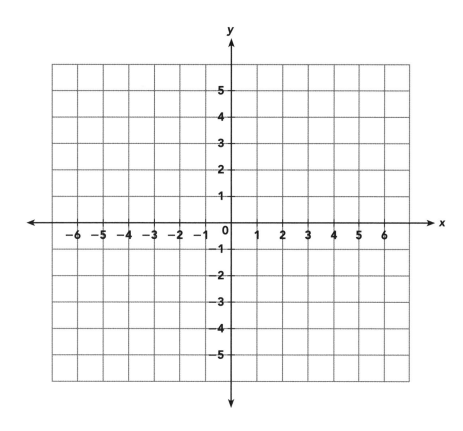

   c) *P'Q'R'S'* can be mapped onto *P"Q"R"S"* by a single transformation in two ways. Describe each of the two ways.

Solve. Show your work.

3. The diagram shows 3 triangles, *P*, *Q*, and *R* on a coordinate plane.

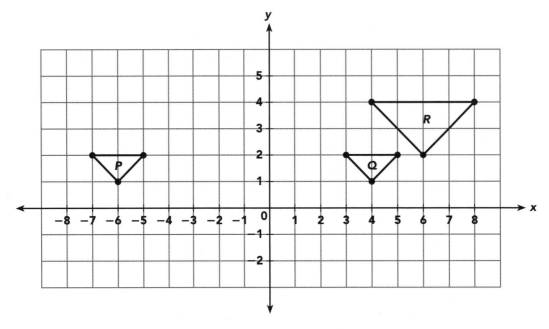

a) Triangle *Q* can be mapped onto triangle *P* by a single transformation
    in two different ways. Describe each of the two ways.

b) Describe the transformation that maps triangle *Q* onto triangle *R*.

Name: _____   Date: _____

Solve. Show your work.

4. Refer to the diagram below. Four triangles are shown on the coordinate plane.

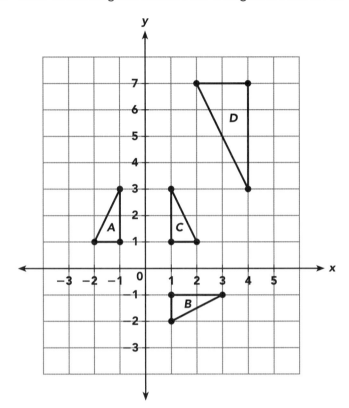

a) Describe the transformation that maps △A onto △B.

b) Describe the transformation that maps △B onto △C.

c) Describe the transformation that maps △A onto △C.

d) Describe the transformation that maps △C onto △D.

Name: _____   Date: _____

Solve. Show your work.

5. The table shows the coordinates for the vertices of four triangles.

△P	△Q	△R	△S
A (3, 4)	A′ (−1, −3)	A″ (−1, −5)	A‴ (−2, −7)
B (−1, 4)	B′ (3, −3)	B″ (3, −5)	B‴ (4, −7)
C (−1, 6)	C′ (3, −5)	C″ (3, −3)	C‴ (4, −4)

a) Draw △P, △Q, △R, and △S.

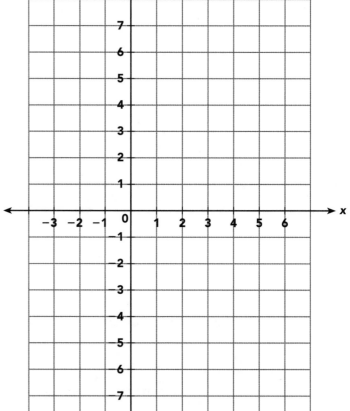

b) Describe two different single transformations that map △P onto △Q.

c) Describe a transformation that maps △Q onto △R.

d) Describe a transformation that maps △R onto △S.

Solve. Show your work.

6. The diagram shows a rhombus. Describe a single transformation (if any) or transformations that map the rhombus onto itself using each of the following:

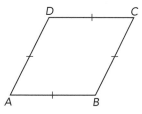

a) Translation

b) Reflection

c) Rotation

d) Dilation

Name: _____   Date: _____

Solve. Show your work.

1. Explain, without the use of a coordinate grid, how you would construct the line of reflection given that *P'* is the image of *P* under the reflection. Show your construction clearly. Then, explain how you would obtain the position of *Q'*, the image of *Q* in the same line of reflection.

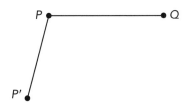

2. The following describes a series of transformation that maps *A* onto *D*:

    A is mapped onto *B*: Translation of 8 units to the right.

    B is mapped onto *C*: Reflection about the *y*-axis.

    C is mapped onto *D*: Rotation of 90° clockwise about the origin.

    Complete the following table to describe a series of transformations that maps *D* onto *A*:

	Transformation
D is mapped onto *C*	
C is mapped onto *B*	
B is mapped onto *A*	

CHAPTER

9 Congruence and Similarity

Lesson 9.1   Understanding and Applying Congruent Figures

Name the figures that are congruent. Name the corresponding congruent line segments and angles.

1. *ABC* is an isosceles triangle and *M* is the midpoint of $\overline{BC}$.

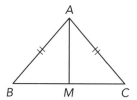

2. *ABCD* is a parallelogram and *AP = CQ*.

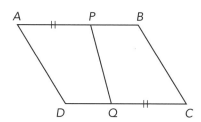

Solve. Show your work.

3. *ABCD* is a kite, whose diagonals intersect at *P*. Name all possible pairs of figures that are congruent. For each pair, name the corresponding congruent line segments and angles.

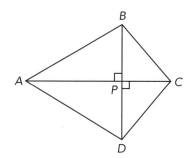

Solve. Show your work.

4. *ABCD* is a rhombus, whose diagonals intersect at *P*. Explain, using a test for congruent triangles, why △*PAB* ≅ △*PCD*.

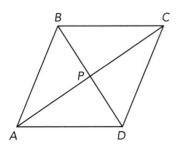

5. *ABCDEF* is a regular hexagon with diagonals $\overline{AC}$, $\overline{AD}$, and $\overline{AE}$ as shown. It is given that $\overline{AC}$ and $\overline{AE}$ are congruent diagonals.

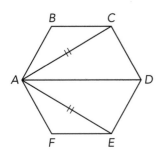

a) Name two pairs of congruent triangles. For each pair, justify the congruency with a test for congruent triangles.

b) Name a pair of congruent quadrilaterals.

Solve. Show your work.

6. In the diagram, $\triangle ABC \cong \triangle DEC$. Find the values of u, v, w, x, y, and z.

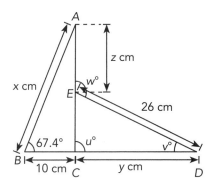

7. $ABCDE \cong QRSTP$. Find the values of u, v, w, x, and y.

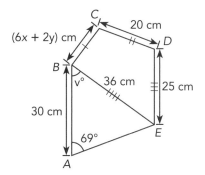
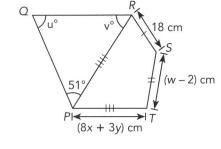

Solve. Show your work.

8. In the diagram, *ABDE* is a parallelogram.
    m∠ACB = m∠DFE = 90°.

    a) Justify that △*ABC* ≅ △*DEF* with a test for congruent triangles.

    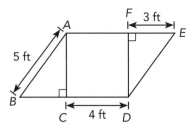

    b) Write the congruence statement for a quadrilateral that is congruent to quadrilateral *ABDF*.

    c) Find the length of each side of the quadrilateral you named in **b)**.

9. In the diagram, *ABCD* is a rhombus and ∠*CDE* = ∠*ADE*.

    a) Identify two pairs of congruent triangles.

    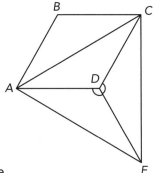

    b) For each pair in **a)**, determine which congruence test proves that the triangles are congruent. Explain.

Lesson 9.2   Understanding and Applying Similar Figures

Identify the figures that seem similar. Explain why.

1.

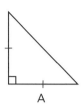
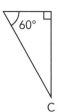

A   B   C   D   E

2.

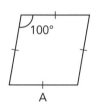
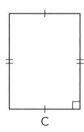
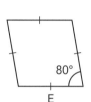

A   B   C   D   E

Triangle *ABC* is similar to triangle *YXZ*. Find the scale factor by which △*ABC* is enlarged to △*YXZ*.

3.

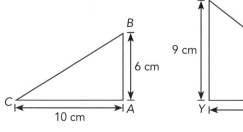

Triangle *ABC* is similar to triangle *XYZ*. Find the scale factor by which △*ABC* is enlarged to △*XYZ*.

4.

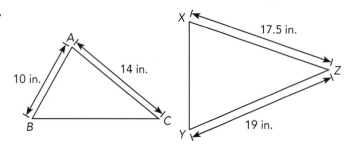

Each pair of figures are similar. Find the value of each variable.

5. △*ABC* ~ △*XYZ*

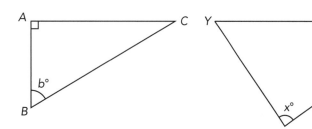

6. △*ABC* ~ △*XYZ*

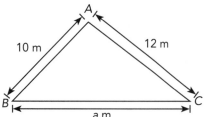 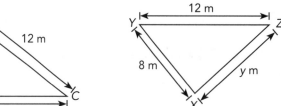

Name: _____   Date: _____

Each pair of figures are similar. Find the value of each variable.

7. △ABC ~ △XYZ

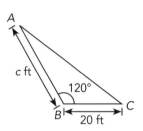

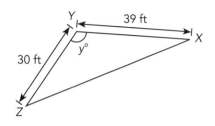

8. ABCD ~ PQRS

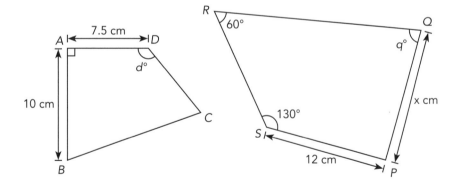

Solve. Show your work.

9. The figure consists of two similar triangles.

    a) Write a statement of similarity of the two triangles.

    b) Explain with a test why the triangles are similar.

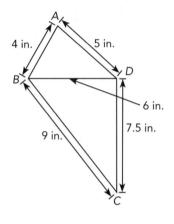

10. The figure shows two similar triangles with m∠BAC = m∠CED.

    a) Write a statement of similarity of the two triangles.

    b) Explain with a test why the triangles are similar.

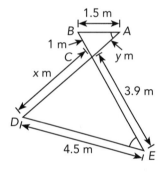

    c) Find the values of unknowns, x and y.

Solve. Show your work.

11. The figure shows two similar triangles with $BE \parallel CD$.

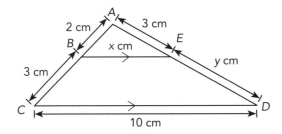

a) Write a statement of similarity of the two triangles.

b) Explain with a test why the triangles are similar.

c) Find the values of the unknowns, x and y.

Solve. Show your work.

12. The figure shows two similar triangles with $BA \parallel DE$.

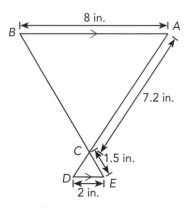

a) Write a statement of similarity of the two triangles.

b) Explain with a test why the triangles are similar.

c) Find the lengths of $\overline{AD}$ and $\overline{BE}$.

Name: _____   Date: _____

Solve. Show your work.

13. The shape shown in Figure A consists of a circle, a square and an equilateral triangle. Figure B and Figure C are photocopies of Figure A.

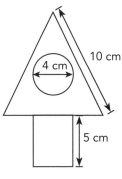

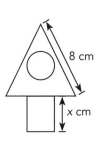

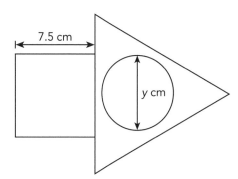

Figure A   Figure B   Figure C

For both Figures B and C:

a) State whether the photocopy is an enlargement or reduction of Figure A.

b) Find the scale factor.

c) Find the values of the unknowns, x and y.

Name: _____   Date: _____

Solve. Show your work.

14. △XYZ is an enlarged copy of △ABC.

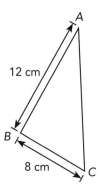

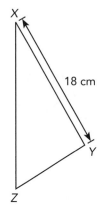

a) Find the scale factor.

b) Find the length of $\overline{YZ}$.

c) If the area of △ABC is 48 square centimeters, find the area of △XYZ.

Solve. Show your work.

15. In the figure, $PQ \parallel XY$.

    a) Find the length of $\overline{XY}$.

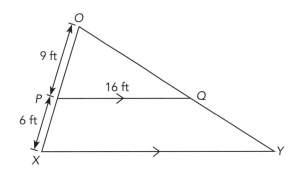

    b) Find the ratio of the area of $\triangle OPQ$ to the area of the trapezoid $PQYX$.

    c) If the area of $\triangle OPQ$ is 80 square feet, find the area of trapezoid $PQYX$.

16. A 6-foot tall man stands $7\frac{1}{2}$ feet from a lamp-post. The lamp at the top of the post casts a shadow of the man on the horizontal ground. If the length of the shadow is $4\frac{1}{2}$ feet, find the height of the lamp-post.

Name: _____   Date: _____

Solve. Show your work.

17. The diagram shows a triangular block with the inner triangle removed.

a) Find the perimeter of the inner triangle removed.

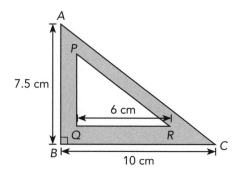

b) Find the area of the remaining block.

18. Two vertical walls, $\overline{AP}$ and $\overline{BQ}$, are supported by poles $\overline{AQ}$ and $\overline{BP}$. Find the length of each pole and the distance between the walls, AB.

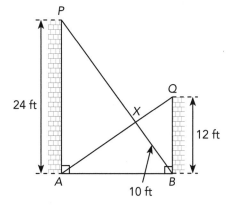

Name: _____   Date: _____

Solve. Show your work.

19. In the diagram, $AB \parallel CD \parallel EF$.

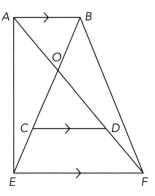

a) Identify three pairs of similar triangles. For each pair, explain why they are similar.

b) Is $\triangle AOE \sim \triangle BOF$? Explain.

Lesson 9.3 Relating Congruent and Similar Figures to Geometric Transformations

State whether each figure and image are congruent or similar.

1. Rectangle *ABCD* is rotated 90° clockwise about vertex *A*.

2. A parallelogram is reflected in the *x*-axis and then reflected in the *y*-axis.

3. A photocopier dilates a picture by a scale factor of $\frac{3}{4}$.

4. A trapezoid is dilated with center (0, 0) and scale factor −1.

5. A hexagon is rotated 90° counterclockwise about its center (0, 0) and then dilated by a scale factor of 2.

6. △*ABC* is mapped onto △*A'B'C'* under a transformation. △*A"B"C"* is the image of △*A'B'C'* under another transformation.

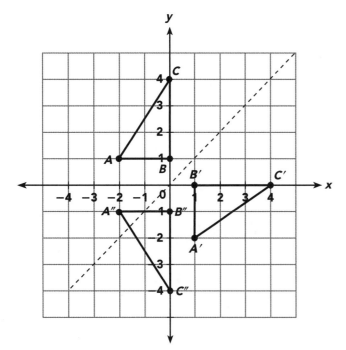

a) Describe the transformations that map △*ABC* onto △*A'B'C'* and △*A'B'C'* onto △*A"B"C"*.

△*ABC* is mapped onto △*A'B'C'* by using a reflection in the line _____.

△*A'B'C'* is mapped onto △*A"B"C"* by using a rotation of _____

about the point (____, ____).

b) If the order of the transformations is reversed, draw △*ABC* and △*A'B'C'* and
△*A"B"C"* on the coordinate plane.

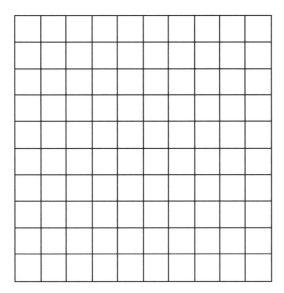

c) Do the two triangles △*A"B"C"* have the same coordinates? Are they
congruent? Explain.

Solve.

7. A triangle *ABC* with vertices *A* (−3, 4), *B* (−3, 2) and *C* (−6, 2) is reflected in the *y*-axis to obtain the image △*A'B'C'*. △*A'B'C'* then is mapped onto △*A"B"C"* shown in the diagram by another transformation.

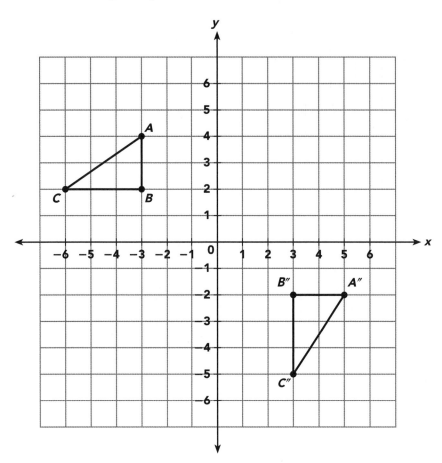

a) Draw △*A'B'C'* on the same axes above.

b) Describe the transformation that maps △*A'B'C'* onto △*A"B"C"*.

c) Describe a single transformation that maps △*ABC* onto △*A"B"C"*.

Solve.

8. A triangle *PQR* with vertices *P* (−2, 2), *Q* (−1, 3), and *R* (−1, 1) is dilated by a scale factor 2 with center *P* to obtain the image △*P'Q'R'*. △*P'Q'R'* is then mapped by another transformation onto △*P"Q"R"* shown in the diagram.

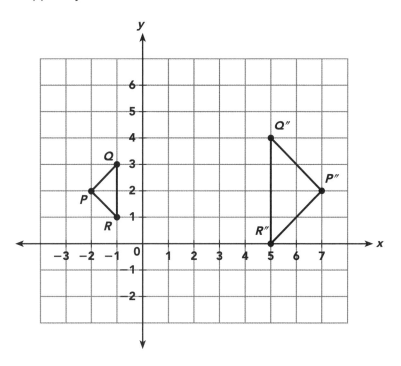

a) Draw △*P'Q'R'* on the same axes above.

b) Describe the transformation that maps △*P'Q'R'* on △*P"Q"R"*.

c) Describe a single transformation that maps △*PQR* onto △*P"Q"R"*.

Solve.

9. △*ABC* is mapped onto △*A'B'C'* under a transformation. △*A'B'C'* is then
    mapped onto △*A"B"C"* under another transformation. Describe the sequence of
    transformations from △*ABC* to △*A"B"C"*.

a)

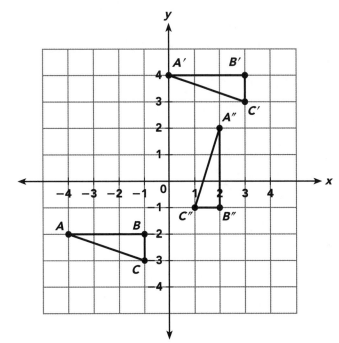

b)

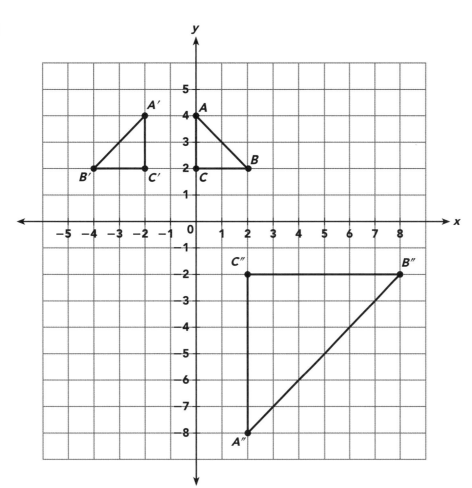

c)

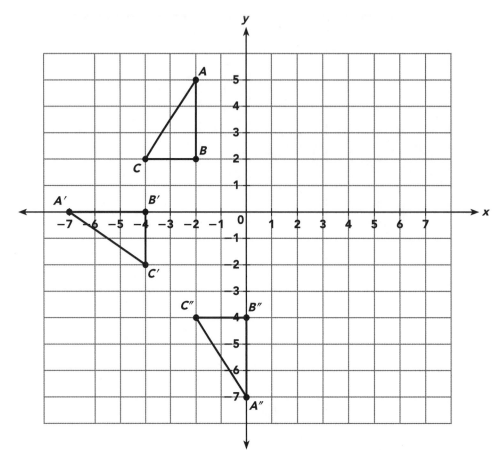

Solve.

10. Quadrilateral *ABCD* is dilated with center *C* and scale factor 1.5. It is mapped onto *PQRS*. The length of $\overline{AB}$ is 3 feet and the area of *ABCD* is 12 square feet.

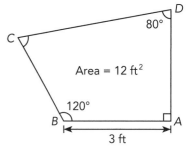

a) Find m∠*QRS*.

b) Find the length of $\overline{PQ}$.

c) Determine the area of *PQRS*.

11. The area of a rectangular postcard is 60 square centimeters. A dilated copy has an area of 240 square centimeters. By what scale factor is the diagonal of the postcard enlarged?

CHAPTER

Brain @ Work

1. Solve for *m* in terms of *n*.

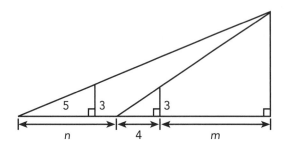

2. In the figure below, *XWZY* is a parallelogram. Show that *AY* : *YZ* = *ZW* : *WB*.

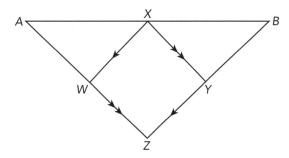

Cumulative Practice
for Chapters 7 to 9

Find the value of each variable. Round your answer to the nearest tenth of a unit when you can.

1.

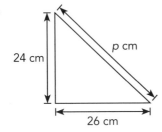

24 cm

p cm

26 cm

2.

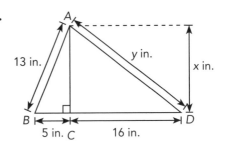

13 in.

y in.

x in.

B

5 in. C

16 in.

D

A

The side lengths of a triangle are given. Decide whether each triangle is a right triangle.

3. 7 ft, 24 ft, 26 ft

4. 7.5 cm, 10 cm, 12.5 cm

Find the distance between each pair of points. Round your answer to the nearest tenth of a unit when you can.

5. E (3, 2), F (5, 11)

6. M (−2, 6), N (4, 0)

For each solid, find the unknown dimension. Round your answer to the nearest tenth of a unit when you can.

7.

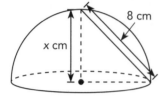

8 cm

x cm

8.

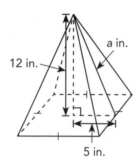

a in.

12 in.

5 in.

Find the volume of each composite solid. Use 3.14 as an approximation of π. If necessary, round your answer to the nearest tenth.

9.

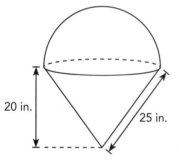

20 in.

25 in.

10.

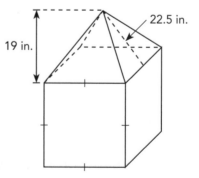

19 in.

22.5 in.

Find the coordinates of the image under each translation.

11. $X(5, -3)$ is translated 3 units to the right and 2 units down.

12. $Y(-8, 7)$ is translated 6 units to the left and 4 units up.

Draw the image under each translation.

13. Rectangle *PQRS* is translated 4 units right and 2 units down.

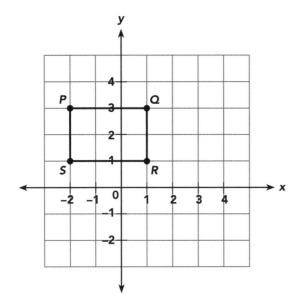

14. Triangle *ABC* is translated 3 units to the left and 2 units up.

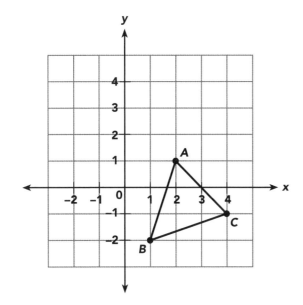

Solve. Show your work.

15. △EFG is shown on the coordinate plane.

    a)   △EFG is mapped onto △KLM under a reflection in the *x*-axis. Draw △KLM.

    b)   △EFG is mapped onto △QRS under a reflection in the *y*-axis. Draw △QRS.

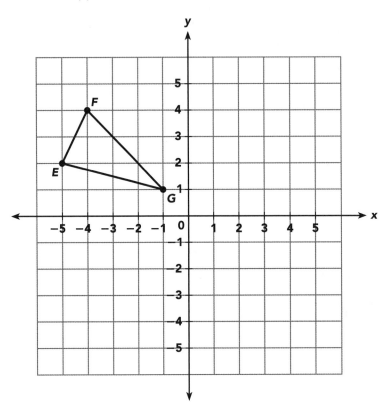

Solve. Show your work.

16. A rotation of point *R* about the origin maps the point onto *R'*. State the angle and direction of the rotation.

a)

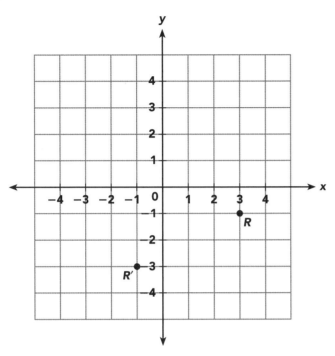

b)

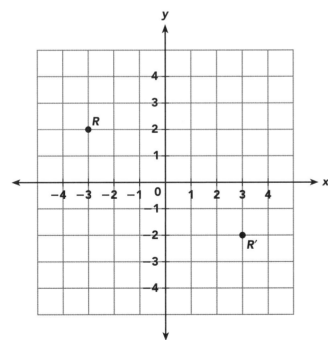

Name: _____   Date: _____

Solve. Show your work.

17. △*ABC* has vertices *A* (−1, 0), *B* (−3, 0), and *C* (−3, 3). Draw the △*ABC* and its image under a rotation of 90° counterclockwise about the origin. Use 1 grid square on both axes to represent 1 unit for the interval from −4 to 4.

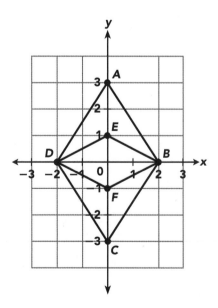

Tell whether each transformation is a dilation. Explain.

18.

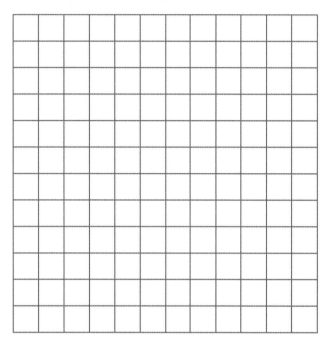

19.

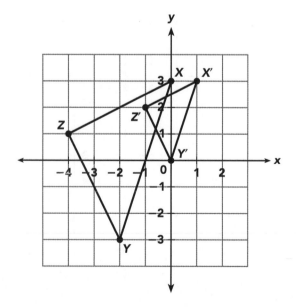

Solve. Show your work.

20. The figure described is mapped onto its image by a dilation with a given point. Draw each figure and its image on the coordinate plane.

   a) The vertices of △PQR are P (4, 5), Q (5, 1), and R (2, 5). △PQR is mapped onto △P'Q'R' with scale factor −1 and center (0, 0).

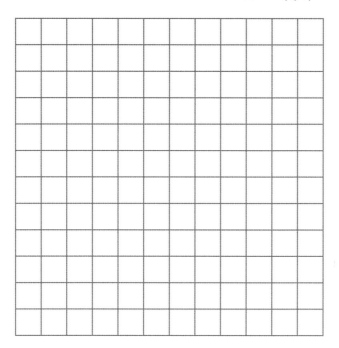

   b) The vertices of square WXYZ are W (2, 1), X (−1, −2), Y (−4, 1), and Z (−1, 4). Square WXYZ is mapped onto W'X'Y'Z' with scale factor $\frac{1}{3}$ and center (5, −5).

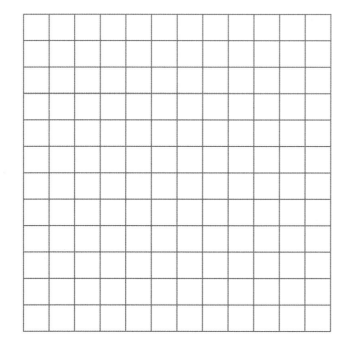

21. Triangle P with vertices (−5, 3), (−4, 5) and (−3, 3) is mapped onto triangle Q. Then triangle Q is mapped onto triangle R as shown on the coordinate plane.

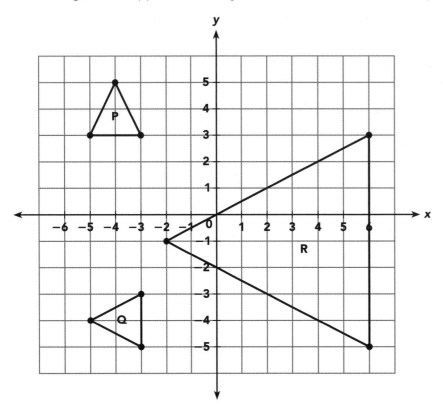

a) Describe the transformation that maps triangle P onto triangle Q.

b) Describe the transformation that maps triangle Q onto triangle R.

Solve. Show your work.

22. State whether the triangles are congruent. If they are congruent, write the statement of congruence and state the test used.

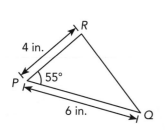

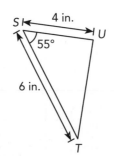

23. △*ABC* is congruent to △*DEF*. Find the values of *x* and *y*.

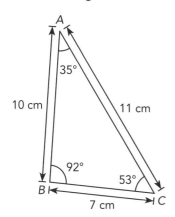

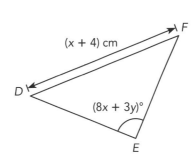

△*GHI* is similar to △*JKL*. Find the value of *p*.

24.

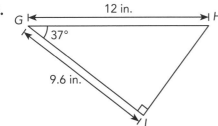

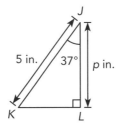

Name the test you can use to determine whether the two triangles are similar. Then find the value of x.

25.

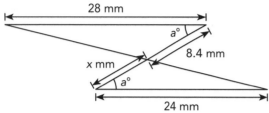

Solve on the coordinate grid.

26. △*PQR* undergoes two transformations to form the image △*P''Q''R''*.

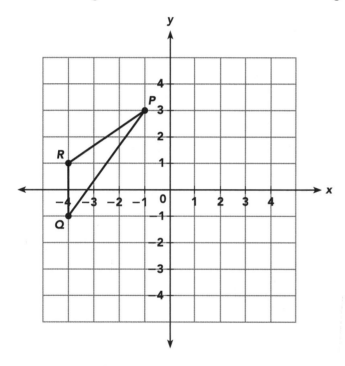

a) What are the coordinates of △*P''Q''R''* if △*PQR* is first reflected in the line
x = 0, and then rotated 90° clockwise about (0, 0)?

b) What are the coordinates of △*P''Q''R''* if △*PQR* is first rotated 90° clockwise
about (0, 0), and then reflected in the line x = 0?

c)   Are the △P″Q″R″ described in **a)** and **b)** congruent? Explain.

d)   Describe a single transformation that maps △PQR to △P″Q″R″ for **a)**.

e)   Describe a single transformation that maps △PQR to △P″Q″R″ for **b)**.

Solve. Show your work.

27. A straw of length 19.5 centimeters is placed in a cylindrical glass of height 18 centimeters. One end of the straw touches the base of the glass and the other end touches the rim of the glass. Find the radius of the glass.

28. The size of a television set is stated as the measure of the length of its diagonal. What is the size of a television set if its length is 33.6 inches and width is 25.2 inches?

© Marshall Cavendish International (Singapore) Private Limited.

Name: _____   Date: _____

Solve. Show your work.

29. The diagram shows two plots of lands, *ABCD* and *HEFG*.

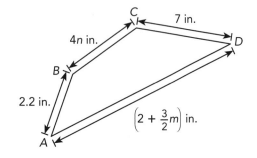 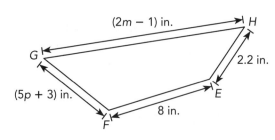

a)   Name the shape congruent to *ABCD*.

b)   Find the values of *m*, *n*, and *p*.

Solve. Show your work.

30. A cone with height 6.2 inches is removed from a cylinder.
    The volume of the cone is 16 cubic inches.

    a)   Find the radius, *r*, of the cone. Use 3.14 as an approximation
         for π. Round your answer to the nearest hundredth.

    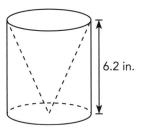

    b)   Find the total surface area of the remaining solid. Round your answer
         to the nearest square inch.

Solve. Show your work.

31. Two pyramids are similar in shape. The bigger pyramid is twice the size of the smaller pyramid. The bigger pyramid has a height of 8 centimeters and a base area of 144 square centimeters.

   a)   Find the slant height of the smaller pyramid.

   b)   Write the ratio of the surface area of the bigger pyramid to the surface area of the smaller pyramid.

Solve. Show your work.

32. A tennis court is 10 centimeters long and 4.6 centimeters wide on a map drawing. The actual length of the tennis court is 78 feet long. What is the actual width of the tennis court if the map drawing is a dilation of the actual court?

Solve. Show your work.

33. Figure *DEFG* is rotated 270° clockwise about *D*. Under this rotation, it is mapped onto figure *STUV*. Figure *STUV* is then dilated with center *S* and a scale factor of −1 onto figure *KHIJ*.

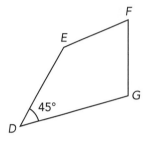

a)   Tell whether *DEFG* and *KHIJ* are congruent or similar figures. Explain.

b)   Find m∠*JST*.

c)   Describe another transformation that maps *STUV* onto *KHIJ*.

CHAPTER

10 Statistics

Lesson 10.1   Scatter Plots

Draw a scatter plot for each table of bivariate data.

1. Use 1 centimeter on the horizontal axis to represent 10 units. Use 1 centimeter on the vertical axis to represent 5 units.

x	20	30	70	80	70	10	60	50
y	10	16	36	40	12	7	30	28

x	40	60	30	70	40	50	40
y	21	31	18	37	20	26	22

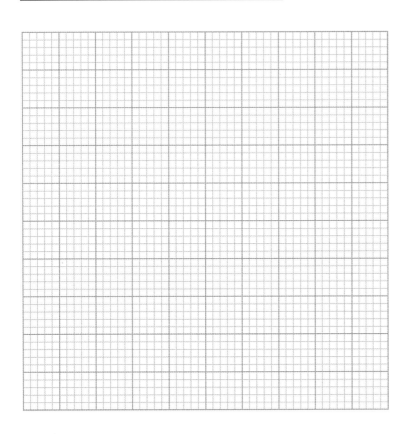

Name: _____   Date: _____

Draw a scatter plot for each table of bivariate data.

2. Use 1 centimeter on the horizontal axis to represent 5 units. Use 1 centimeter on the vertical axis to represent 10 units.

u	10	5	40	20	25	15	10	20
v	21	91	21	60	50	68	79	59

u	15	35	30	15	20	35	25	30
v	71	31	39	48	62	30	51	38

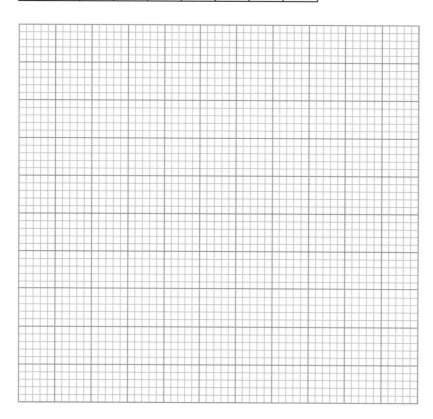

Draw a scatter plot for each table of bivariate data.

3. Use 1 centimeter on the horizontal axis to represent 10 seconds. Use 1 centimeter on the vertical axis to represent 5 meters per second.

Time (*t* seconds)	40	60	80	20	30	50	70	80
Speed (*v* meters per second)	23	16	13	50	34	19	14	12

Time (*t* seconds)	30	40	70	50	40	70	90
Speed (*v* meters per second)	32	24	15	21	26	16	10

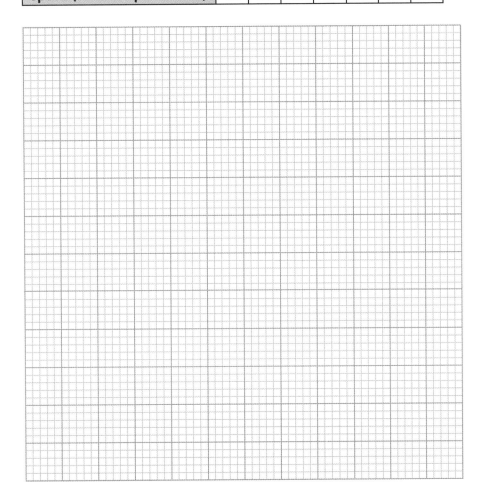

Name: _____   Date: _____

Describe the association shown in the bivariate data for each scatter plot.

4.

5.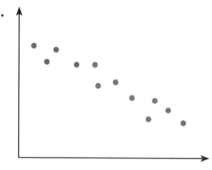

6.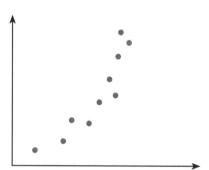

7.

Identify the outlier(s) in the scatter plot.

8.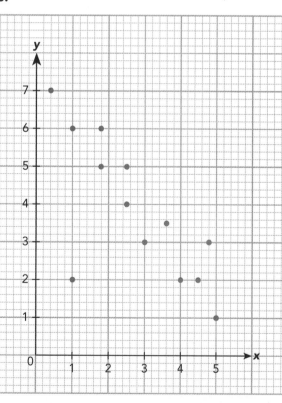

9.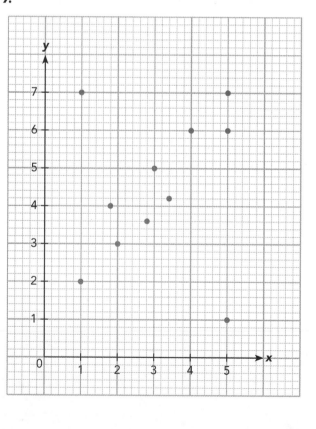

Use the table of bivariate data below to answer questions 10 to 12.

The table show the time spent in batting practice y hours, as it relates to the number of games won, x, for a softball team over 16 seasons.

Number of Games Won (x)	5	3	5	1	1	3	7	3	2	4
Number of Practice Hours (y hours)	140	100	150	80	90	120	150	130	90	130

Mass (m kilograms)	8	6	2	0	3	6	1	4	5	2
Height (h centimeters)	160	140	100	90	110	150	160	120	130	110

10. Use the graph paper on the next page. Construct the scatter plot. Use 1 centimeter on the horizontal axis to represent 1 game for the x interval from 0 to 10. Use 1 centimeter on the vertical axis to represent 10 hours for the y interval from 80 to 160.

11. Identify the outlier. Give a likely explanation for the occurrence of the outlier.

12. Describe the association between the heights and masses of the students. Explain your answer.

Name: _____ Date: _____

Name: _____ Date: _____

A teacher instructing a Mathematics course recorded the student scores for a midterm and a final exam.

Midterm Score (x points)	34	54	54	80	86	60	42	70	51	85
Final Exam Score (y points)	44	66	70	78	42	60	53	68	52	80

Midterm Score (x points)	93	38	34	88	47	30	54	75	65	48
Final Exam Score (y points)	89	34	41	85	41	36	62	75	64	60

13. Use the graph paper on the next page. Construct the scatter plot. Use 1 centimeter on both axes to represent 10 points.

14. Identify the outlier. Give a likely explanation of the occurrence of the outlier.

15. Describe the association between the points scored on the midterm and those scored on the final exam. Explain your answer.

Lesson 10.2   Modeling Linear Associations

State the line that represents a line of best fit for each scatter plot.

1.

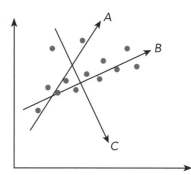

2.

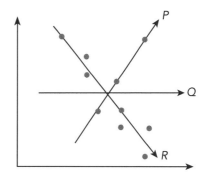

Draw a scatter plot and a line of best fit for each table of bivariate data.

3. Use 1 centimeter on the horizontal axis to represent 0.1 unit for the interval 0 to 1.0. Use 1 centimeter on the vertical axis to represent 5 units.

x	0.4	0.5	0.4	0.7	0.3	0.6	0.4
y	17	21	14	30	13	25	19

x	0.5	0.6	0.5	0.8	0.7	0.3	0.2
y	20	23	8	36	29	10	6

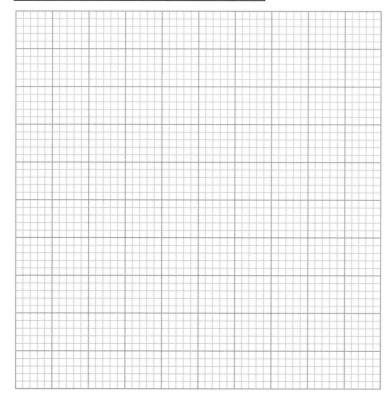

Draw a scatter plot and a line of best fit for each table of bivariate data.

4. Use 1 centimeter on the horizontal axis to represent 10 units. Use 1 centimeter on the vertical axis to represent 10 units.

u	60	50	70	40	30	60	70	30
v	28	40	20	53	30	31	22	60

u	40	20	30	50	40	80	20
v	48	70	58	44	52	12	72

Draw a scatter plot and a line of best fit for each table of bivariate data.

5. Use 1 centimeter on the horizontal axis to represent 1 second. Use 1 centimeter on the vertical axis to represent 10 meters.

Time (*t* seconds)	7	5	4	1	8	3	2	9
Distance (*d* meters)	76	59	51	20	92	40	32	98

Time (*t* seconds)	7	5	4	6	2	3	5
Distance (*d* meters)	82	62	81	72	20	44	58

Name: _____   Date: _____

Draw a scatter plot and a line of best fit for each table of bivariate data.
Find the equation of the line of best fit.

6. Use 1 centimeter on the horizontal axis to represent 1 worker for the x interval from 20 to 30. Use 1 centimeter on the vertical axis to represent 10 items produced for the y interval from 170 to 280.

Number of Workers (x)	24	23	30	21	28	25	30
Number of Items Produced (y)	210	202	196	176	246	222	274

Number of Workers (x)	27	27	26	23	29	26
Number of Items Produced (y)	270	242	230	198	256	240

**Draw a scatter plot and a line of best fit for each table of bivariate data.
Find the equation of the line of best fit.**

7. Use 1 centimeter on the horizontal axis to represent 1 item for the *x* interval
from 50 to 60. Use 1 centimeter on the vertical axis to represent $5 for the
y interval from 10 to 50.

Number of Items Assembled (*x*)	53	59	57	50	54	56	51
Cost Per Item (*y* dollars)	40	25	30	50	38	33	48

Number of Items Assembled (*x*)	56	52	55	60	58	55
Cost Per Item (*y* dollars)	32	30	37	18	26	38

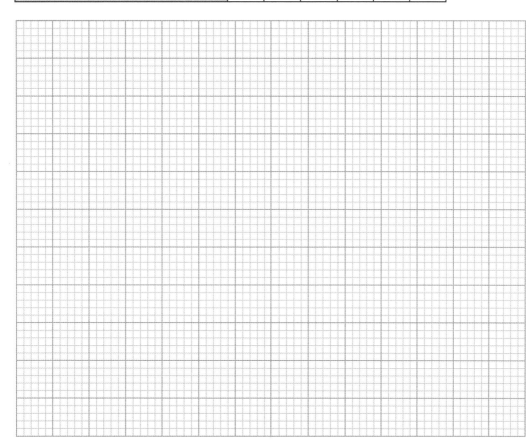

Use the table below in question 8 to answer questions 9 to 14.

To understand the relationship between area of living space within a home, x square feet, and cost of electricity, y dollars, data are collected for a particular month and recorded.

Area of Living Space (x square feet)	1,400	1,000	1,300	1,100	1,500	1,300
Electricity Cost (y dollars)	210	200	226	206	258	228

Area of Living Space (x square feet)	1,200	1,100	1,400	1,200	1,400
Electricity Cost (y dollars)	223	212	242	215	246

8. Use the graph paper on the next page. Construct the scatter plot. Use 1 centimeter on the horizontal axis to represent 100 square feet for the x interval from 1,000 to 1,500. Use 2 centimeters on the vertical axis to represent $10 for the y interval from 200 to 260.

9. Sketch a line of best fit.

10. Find an equation for the line of best fit.

11. Describe the association between area of living space within a home and cost of electricity.

12. Identify the outlier. Give a likely explanation of the occurrence of the outlier.

13. Use the graph to predict the cost for electricity for a 1,350 square-foot home.

14. Use the graph in **question 9** to predict the area of living space within a home given an electricity cost of $230.

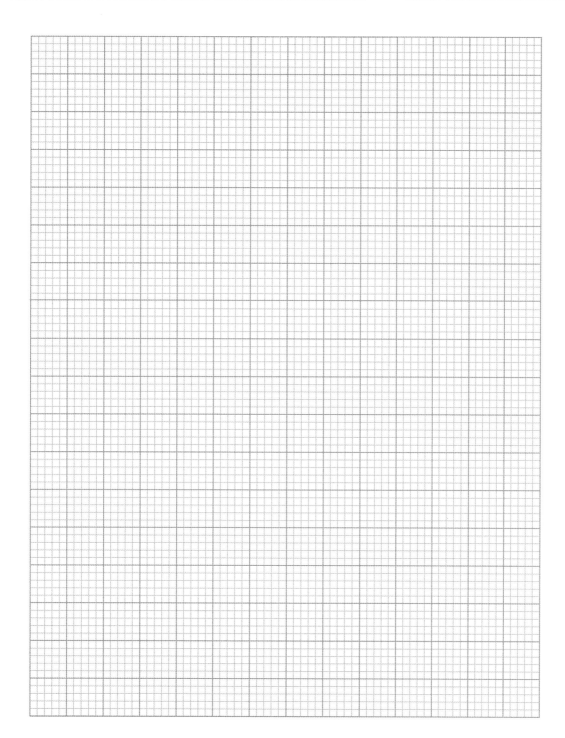

Lesson 10.3   Two-Way Tables

Identify the categorical data.

1. Height, Hobby, Capacity

2. Mass, Velocity, Color

Identify whether the given data is categorical or quantitative.

3. Fast, Moderate, Slow

4. 5 points, 15 points, 20 points

5. 3rd game, 5th game, 9th game

Use the two-way table to answer questions 6 to 8.

A standardized assessment in two subjects, Mathematics and Science, was given to 160 students. Some of the assessment results are shown in the two-way table.

Results for Mathematics

		Pass	Fail	Total
Results for Science	**Pass**	x	5	125
	Fail	25	y	t
	Total	145	15	160

6. Find the number of students who passed both Mathematics and Science, x.

7. Find the number of students who failed both Mathematics and Science, y.

8. Find the number of students who failed Science, t.

Use the data collected to answer questions 9 to 11.

A survey was carried out on 30 members of a sports club to find out if they play basketball and volleyball. The results are as follows:

Plays Basketball	B	NB	B	B	NB	B	NB	NB	B	NB	B	NB	NB	B	NB
Plays Volleyball	NV	V	NV	V	V	NV	NV	V	NV	V	V	V	V	NV	V

Plays Basketball	NB	B	B	NB	B	NB	B	NB	B	NB	NB	NB	NB	NB	B
Plays Volleyball	V	NV	NV	V	NV	V	V	V	NV	V	V	NV	V	V	NV

Key: B represents play basketball. NB represents does not play basketball.
   V represents play volleyball. NV represents does not play volleyball.

9. Construct a two-way table to display the data.

10. Which of the following is true? Explain.
   • Most of the members play both games.
   • Most of the members play one of the two games.
   • Most of the members play neither game

11. Is there any association between the club members who play basketball and those who play volleyball? Explain.

Use the table to answer questions 12 to 14.

The two-way table shows the type of chess that randomly selected high-school chess club participants play.

Plays International Chess

		Yes	No	Total
Plays Chinese Chess	**Yes**	40	2	42
	No	3	5	8
	Total	43	7	50

12. Find the relative frequencies among the rows, and interpret their meanings. Round your answer to the nearest hundredth where necessary.

13. Find the relative frequencies within each column, and interpret their meanings. Round your answer to the nearest hundredth where necessary.

14. Describe the association between a high-school chess club participant who plays Chinese Chess and one who plays International Chess.

Name: _____   Date: _____

Jenny constructs two scatter plots. One displays bivariate data on x and y. The other displays bivariate data on x and z. The equation of the line of best fit for the first scatter plot is $y = x$, and the equation of the line of best fit for the second scatter plot is $z = 3x + 2$. Jenny concludes that there is a linear association between y and z. Explain.

CHAPTER

Probability

Lesson 11.1   Compound Events

Tell whether each statement is True or False.

1. Selecting a vowel from the alphabet is a simple event.

2. Getting a six when throwing 2 fair six-sided number dice is a simple event.

3. Getting two heads when tossing 2 coins is a compound event.

4. Selecting a ball labeled 1 from a bag containing 10 balls labeled 1 to 10 is a compound event.

Tell whether each event is a simple or compound event. If it is a compound event, identify the simple events that form the compound event.

5. Selecting the letter M from the word GEOMETRY

6. Drawing a black pebble followed by a white pebble from a bag containing 5 black pebbles and 5 white pebbles

7. Drawing a picture card from an ordinary deck of 52 playing cards

8. Rolling a fair four-sided die twice and obtaining a product of 6

Solve. Show your work.

9. A spinner with three equal sectors labeled 1 to 3 is spun and a fair six-sided number die is rolled.

   a) Draw a possibility diagram to represent the possible outcomes.

   b) How many possible outcomes are there?

10. Jane plays a game involving a regular tetrahedral die and a bag of tiles. The die has four faces labeled A, B, C, and D, and the bag contains 6 titles labeled Q, W, E, R, T, and Y.

    The die is rolled and the spinner is spun, and the results on each are recorded.

    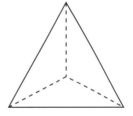

    a) Draw a possibility diagram to represent the possible outcomes.

    b) How many possible outcomes are there?

Name: _____   Date: _____

Solve. Show your work.

11. A bag contains 2 white golf balls and 1 green golf ball. Another bag contains
1 red cube and 2 yellow cubes. Alan draws a ball from the first bag and a cube
from the second bag.

   a) Use a tree diagram to represent the possible outcomes for drawing a ball
   and a cube.

   b) How many possible outcomes are there?

Solve. Show your work.

12. A desk drawer contains 2 red, 2 green, and 2 silver paperclips, and 1 black and 2 yellow permanent markers. Ben reaches into the drawer and randomly selects a paperclip and a permanent marker. Use a tree diagram to represent the possible outcomes. Then tell the number of possible outcomes.

Solve. Show your work.

13. A fair six-sided number die and a fair four-sided number die are tossed at the same time and the sum is recorded.

    a) Draw a possibility diagram to show the possible outcomes. Then find the number of favorable outcomes for an even sum.

    b) Use the possibility diagram to find the number of favorable outcomes for a sum greater than 6.

    c) Which event is more likely: having a prime number sum or having a composite number sum?

Solve. Show your work.

14. Tory randomly selected a digit from his locker combination: 1-2-5-6-3-4 and randomly selected a digit from his computer password: 2-6-1-5-4-3. The product of the numbers were recorded.

    a) Draw a possibility diagram to show the possible outcomes.

    b) Use the possibility diagram to find the number of favorable outcomes for a product greater than 20.

    c) Use the possibility diagram to find the number of favorable outcomes for an odd product.

Lesson 11.2   Probability of Compound Events

Solve. Show your work.

1. Bag A contains 1 blue marble and 3 green marbles. Bag B contains 3 blue
    marbles and 1 green marble. Charlie randomly draws a marble from Bag A and
    another marble from Bag B. Use a possibility diagram to find the probability
    that the marbles are of different colors.

2. A letter is randomly chosen from the word BELL, and another letter is chosen
    randomly from the word BEEP. Draw a tree diagram to represent all the
    possible outcomes. Then find the probability that both letters chosen are the
    same.

Solve. Show your work.

3. Three colored pens are placed in a backpack, 1 pen with black ink and 2 pens with green ink. First, Peter randomly selects a pen from the backpack. Then he rolls a fair six-sided number die labeled from 1 to 6. The result recorded is the number facing up. Draw a possibility diagram to represent all the possible outcomes. Then find the probability of selecting a green pen and getting an even number.

4. Tina rolled a red fair four-sided number die and a yellow fair four-sided number die, each with faces labeled 1 to 4. The results recorded are the numbers facing down. Draw a possibility diagram to represent all the possible outcomes. Then find the probability that the sum of the numbers is at least 6.

Name: _____ Date: _____

Solve. Show your work.

5. A shop sells 3 brands of apple juice, 2 brands of grape juice, and 1 brand of orange juice. The juices are sold in small, medium, and large bottles. A customer randomly selects a bottle of fruit juice. Draw a possibility diagram to represent all the possible outcomes. Then find the probability that the customer selects a small bottle of apple juice.

6. Anna draws a bead from three numbered beads: 1, 3, and 5. Then she randomly selects a card from four number cards: 1, 2, 4, and 6. The product of the numbers drawn is recorded.

    a) Draw a possibility diagram to represent all the possible outcomes.

    b) Find the probability of getting a product that is greater than or equal to 5, and less than or equal to 10.

Solve. Show your work.

7. Bucket A contains a blue hermit crab, a green hermit crab, and a red hermit crab. Bucket B contains a green pebble, a red pebble, and a yellow pebble. Paulette randomly selects a hermit crab from Bucket A and a pebble from Bucket B. Draw a possibility diagram to represent all the possible outomes. Then find the probability that the crab and the pebble are the same color.

8. Jimmy randomly draws a disc from a bag containing 2 blue discs and 1 red disc. He then rolls a fair four-sided number die labeled 1, 1, 3, and 4, and records the result. The result recorded is the number facing down. Draw a possibility diagram to represent all the possible outcomes. Then find the probability of drawing a blue disc and getting a 1.

Solve. Show your work.

9. One red tissue and one black tissue are placed in a basket. Rudy randomly
    selects a tissue and notes its color. After replacing the tissue, Rudy randomly
    selects another tissue and notes its color. This process is repeated a third time.
    Draw a tree diagram to represent all the possible outcomes. Then find the
    probability that Rudy selected the red tissue more times than the black tissue.

10. Jessica writes a letter to each of her three friends. She writes each address on
    three different envelopes. She then randomly inserts the letters into the three
    different envelopes. Draw a possibility diagram to represent all the possible
    outcomes. Then find the probability that all of the letters correspond to the
    correct envelope.

Lesson 11.3   Independent Events

Draw a tree diagram to represent each situation.

1. Popping a balloon randomly from a centerpiece consisting of 1 black balloon and 1 white balloon, followed by tossing a fair six-sided number die

2. Randomly selecting a marble, replacing it, and randomly selecting a marble again from a bag containing 1 black marble, 1 green marble, and 1 red marble

3. Drawing a bead randomly from a bag containing 1 black bead, 1 white bead, 1 green bead, and 1 red bead, followed by tossing a fair coin

Draw a tree diagram to represent each compound event.

4. Randomly drawing three tokens, and replacing each one before the next draw, from a bag containing one $2 token and one $5 token

5. Recording the weather outcome for each day as either rain or shine for four consecutive days, assuming that each outcome is equally likely

6. Randomly choosing a mode of transportation from bus, car, or train, on Saturday and Sunday, assuming all are equally likely

Solve. Show your work.

7. A game is played using a fair coin and a fair six-sided number die. An outcome of heads on the coin and 5 or 6 on the die wins the game.

a) Draw a tree diagram to represent the possible outcomes of this game.

b) Find the probability of winning the game in one try.

c) Find the probability of losing the game in one try.

Solve. Show your work.

8. There are 2 green party hats and 3 red party hats on a table. Ken randomly selects a party hat from the table. He tries the hat on, and then places it back on the table. He randomly selects another party hat.

   a) Draw a tree diagram to represent the possible outcomes.

   b) Find the probability that Ken selects 2 red party hats.

   c) Find the probability that Ken selects a red party hat after he first selects a green party hat.

Name: _____   Date: _____

Solve. Show your work.

9. Alice has 1 green bead, 2 red beads, and 3 yellow beads in her bag. She randomly selects a bead from her bag, and replaces it before she randomly selects again.

   a) Draw a tree diagram to represent the possible outcomes.

   b) Find the probability that she selects 2 red beads.

   c) Find the probability that she selects 2 yellow beads.

   d) Find the probability she selects 2 beads of different colors.

Solve. Show your work.

10. A box contains 2 blue cards, 3 red cards, and 5 yellow cards. Tom randomly selects a card from the box, and replaces it before he randomly selects again.

    a) Draw a tree diagram to represent the possible outcomes.

    b) Find the probability that he selects 2 red cards.

    c) Find the probability that he selects a blue card, followed by a yellow card.

    d) Find the probability that he selects a yellow card, followed by a red card.

Name: _____   Date: _____

Solve. Show your work.

11. James has two fair six-sided number dice, one white and one red. He tosses the red die followed by the white die.

   a) Find the probability of tossing an odd number on both dice.

   b) Find the probability of tossing an odd number on the red die and an even number on the white die.

   c) Find the probability of tossing a number greater than 4 on both dice.

12. The probability of Nancy getting to school on time on any given day, is $\frac{9}{10}$. What is the probability of Nancy getting to school late on at least one of any two consecutive days?

13. A spinner has a 60° green sector, a 120° blue sector, and a 180° red sector. Henry spins the spinner twice.

   a) Find the probability that the spinner points to the same color on both spins.

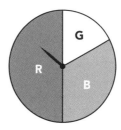

   b) Find the probability that the spinner points to the blue sector at least once.

Solve. Show your work.

14. A game is designed so that a player wins when the game piece lands on or passes the box W. The game piece starts on box S. A fair six-sided number die is tossed. If the number tossed is 1 or 2, the game piece stays put. If the number tossed is 3 or 4, the game piece moves one box to the right. If the number tossed is 5 or 6, the game piece moves two boxes to the right.

S		W		

a) Find the probability that a player will win after tossing the die once.

b) Find the probability that a player will win after tossing the die twice.

15. A target board consists of two concentric circles with radii of 3 inches and 6 inches. Chrissy thinks that the probability of tossing a coin and it landing on the shaded part is $\frac{1}{2}$ since $OA = AB = 3$ inches. Do you agree with her? Explain.

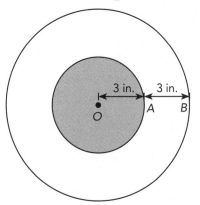

Lesson 11.4   Dependent Events

State whether each pair of events is dependent or independent.

1. Drawing 2 green marbles randomly, one at a time without replacement, from a bag containing 10 blue marbles and 10 green marbles

2. Tossing a fair six-sided number die twice

3. Selecting 2 balloons at random from a bouquet of ordinary colored balloons

4. Tossing a coin three times

Draw a tree diagram for each situation.

5. Two beads are drawn at random, one at a time without replacement, from a bag of 2 blue beads and 3 red beads.

6. The probability that it rains on a particular day is $\frac{1}{4}$. If it rains, then the probability that it rains the next day is $\frac{1}{3}$. If it does not rain, then the probability that it does not rain the next day is $\frac{3}{5}$.

Name: _____ Date: _____

Solve. Show your work.

7. Gerald has a bag of 10 colored balls: 3 green, 3 red, and the rest yellow. He randomly draws two balls, one at a time without replacement.

   a) Find the probability of drawing 2 red balls.

   b) Find the probability of drawing at least 1 yellow ball.

8. A bag contains 2 black socks, 4 red socks, and 6 white socks. Linda randomly picks two socks from the bag, one at a time without replacement.

   a) Find the probability that the socks are of the same color.

   b) Find the probability that the socks are of different colors.

Solve. Show your work.

9. There are 12 picture cards, 20 red cards, and 20 black cards in a deck. Jack and Jill each randomly pick a card from the deck. Jack picks a card first before Jill picks.

   a) Find the probability that Jack and Jill both pick picture cards.

   b) Find the probability that Jack picks a red card and Jill a black card, or vice versa.

10. The probability diagram shows the probability of rain on two consecutive days. The probability of rain on a particular day is denoted by x.

    a) If $x = \frac{1}{3}$, what are the values of y and z? Find the probability that it rains exactly one of the two days.

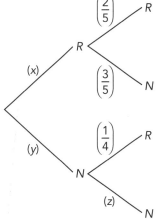

1st Day   2nd Day

R represents rain
N represents no rain

    b) If the probability of it raining on both days is $\frac{3}{10}$, find the values of x and y.

Solve. Show your work.

11. A fruit basket contains 3 apples, 4 oranges, and 5 pears. Peter and Paul each randomly select a fruit from the basket.

a) Draw a tree diagram to represent the outcomes.

b) Find the probability that Peter selects an apple and Paul selects a pear.

c) Find the probability that Peter and Paul both select the same type of fruit.

d) Find the probability that an orange is selected by either Peter or Paul.

Solve. Show your work.

12. Among a group of 15 students, 4 have blue eyes, 5 have green eyes, and the rest have brown eyes. Two of the students are randomly selected, one after another, to use the class computer.

a) Draw a tree diagram to represent the possible outcomes.

b) What is the probability that the first student selected has brown eyes?

c) What is the probability that the first student selected has blue eyes, followed by a student with green eyes?

d) What is the probability that both the students selected have eyes of the same color?

Solve. Show your work.

13. A bag contains 12 nuts: x are almonds and the rest are walnuts. Mary randomly
selects and eats a nut, followed by Nancy.

a) If the probability that Mary eats an almond is $\frac{1}{3}$, find the value of x.

b) Draw a tree diagram to show the possible outcomes.

c) What is the probability that Mary and Nancy both eat the
same type of nut?

Solve. Show your work.

14. Alan and Bob play a game. The probability that Alan wins a particular game is 0.6. If he wins, the probability that he wins the next game is x. If he loses, the probability that he wins the next game is 0.5.

   a) If the probability that Alan wins both games is 0.42, what is the value of x?

   b) Draw a tree diagram to show the possible outcomes.

   c) What is the probability that Bob wins both games?

   d) What is the probability that Bob wins at least one of the games?

CHAPTER

11 Brain @ Work

1. In tennis, a player is allowed a second serve if their first serve is a fault. Dominic has a first serve which wins him 75% of the points if it is not a fault, but he only succeeds in getting it in play one out of four times. His second serve is not a fault three out of five times, but he only wins 55% of the subsequent points. What percentage of points can Dominic expect to win when he is serving?

2. An integer between one and one million inclusive is randomly chosen.

   a) Find the probability that it is not a perfect square.

   b) The probability of obtaining a prime number between one and one million is approximately 7.24%. Find the approximate number of primes between one and one million.

Cumulative Practice
for Chapters 10 and 11

Draw a scatter plot for each table of bivariate data. Identify any outliers.

1. Use 1 centimeter on the horizontal axis to represent 10 units and 1 centimeter on the vertical axis to represent 5 units.

x	40	50	40	70	30	60	40	50	60	10	70	80	70	30	20
y	10	16	36	40	12	7	30	28	21	32	18	37	20	26	22

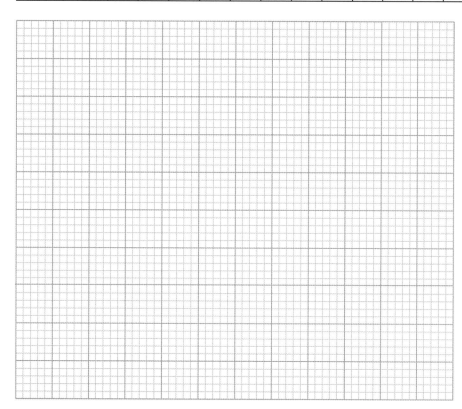

Draw a scatter plot for each table of bivariate data. Identify any outliers.

2. Use 1 centimeter to represent 10 units on both axes.

x	50	30	20	40	30	70	60	30	40	70	50	60	40	80	20
y	37	22	11	33	20	58	48	50	30	50	40	52	28	68	8

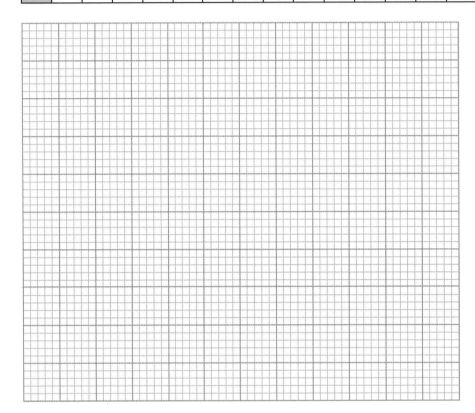

Describe the association between the bivariate data shown in each scatter plot.

3.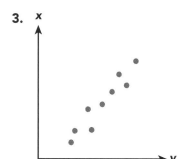

4.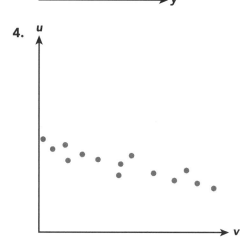

State the line that represents the line of best fit for the scatter plot.

5.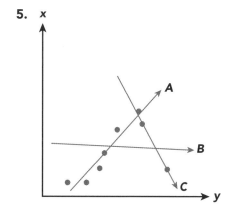

Name: _____   Date: _____

Draw the scatter plot and a line of best fit for the given table of bivariate data.

6. Use 1 centimeter to represent 10 units on both axes.

Number of Songs Downloaded (x)	50	20	40	10	60	20	30	80	70	30	50	40	60	70
Total Downloading Fees (y dollars)	88	39	78	21	111	81	40	148	130	48	92	81	60	126

Draw the scatter plot and a line of best fit for the given table of bivariate data.

7. Use 1 centimeter on the horizontal axis to represent 10 units and 1 centimeter on the vertical axis to represent 5 units.

Number of Goods Purchased (x)	10	30	60	70	50	80	20	40	70	20	40	50
Shipping Charges ($)	15	24	41	44	34	49	21	30	47	19	31	36

Identify whether the given data are qualitative or quantitative.

8. Small, medium, large

9. 2 cm, 3 m, 4 km

Complete the two-way table. Then use the table to answer each question.

10. Potential college students were surveyed to find out if they prefer guided or self-guided tours when visiting a college campus. The results of the survey are shown in the two-way table.

Tour Preference

		Guided	Self-Guided	Total
Gender	**Male**		8	11
	Female	5		9
	Total			20

a) Find the number of males who prefer guided tours.

b) Find the number of females who prefer self-guided tours.

c) Find the number of potential college students who prefer guided tours.

d) Find the number of potential college students who prefer self-guided tours.

Construct a two-way table using the given data.

11. Twenty people in a park were asked if they prefer to cycle or walk for exercise. The results of the survey are shown in the table.

Cycle	NC	C	NC	NC	C	C	NC	NC	C	NC
Walk	W	W	NW	W	NW	W	W	W	NW	W

Cycle	C	NC	C	NC	C	C	NC	NC	NC	C
Walk	W	W	NW	W	NW	W	W	W	W	W

C represents cycling for exercise
NC represents not cycling for exercise
W represents walking for exercise
NW represents not walking for exercise

Tell whether the outcomes described are from a simple or compound event. State the single event or identify the simple events that form the compound event.

12. Getting an even number when rolling a fair six-sided number die

13. Drawing an A-tile, followed by another A-tile from a bag of tiles containing the seven letters in ALABAMA

Name: _____   Date: _____

Solve. Show your work.

14. Draw a possibility diagram to represent the possible outcomes when Spinners A and B are spun. Then find the total number of possible outcomes.

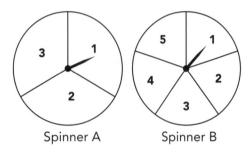

Spinner A   Spinner B

15. Spinner R is divided into 3 equal areas and labeled red, blue, and yellow. The spinner is spun twice.

   a) Draw a tree diagram to represent the possible outcomes.

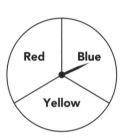

Spinner R

   b) State the total number of possible outcomes.

Name: _____   Date: _____

Solve. Show your work.

16. The table shows the mass, x grams, of a chemical reactant as it relates to the amount of time taken to complete a chemical reaction, y minutes.

Mass (x grams)	2.5	4	5	3.5	3	2.5	4	3	2	3.5	1
Time (y minutes)	3.8	2.9	2.5	3.2	3.5	2.9	3.0	3.6	4.2	3.4	4.6

a) Construct a scatter plot for the data. Use 1 centimeter on both axes to represent 0.5 unit.

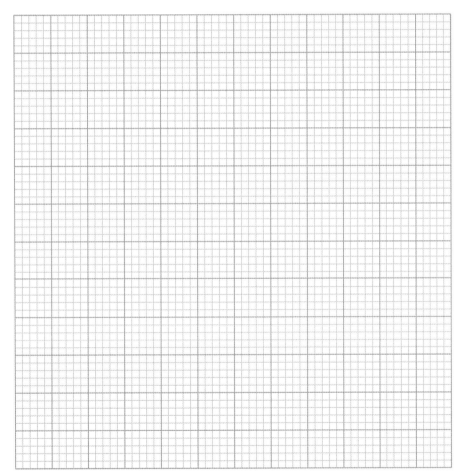

b) Identify the outliers.

c) On the scatter plot in **a)**, draw the line of best fit. Then write the equation of the line of best fit.

Name: _____ Date: _____

Solve. Show your work.

17. The table shows a farm's annual potato yield, y tons per acre, as it relates to the amount of annual rainfall, x inches per year.

Rainfall (x inches/year)	13	11	12	14	15	14	10	16	13	12
Yield (y tons/acre)	7.2	5.8	6.5	7.6	8.1	7.2	5.5	8.4	6.9	6.4

a) Construct a scatter plot for the data. Use 1 centimeter on the horizontal axis to represent 1 inch for the x interval from 10 to 16. Use 1 centimeter on the vertical axis to represent 0.5 tons per acre for the y interval from 5 to 8.5.

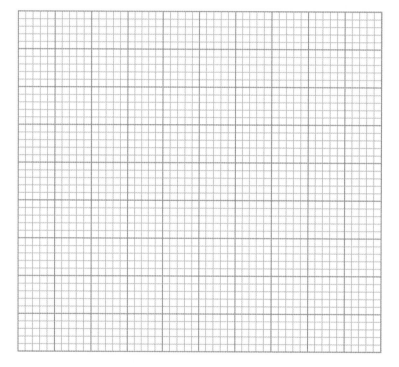

b) On the scatter plot in **a)**, draw the line of best fit. Then write the equation of the line of best fit.

c) Estimate the annual potato yield when the annual rainfall is $14\frac{1}{2}$ inches.

Solve. Show your work.

18. In Bag A, there is 1 red ball and 1 yellow ball. In Bag B, there is 1 blue cube, 1 red cube, and 1 yellow cube. A ball is randomly drawn from Bag A, and then a cube is randomly drawn from Bag B.

  a) Draw a possibility diagram to represent the possible outcomes.

  b) What is the probability that objects drawn are of the same color?

19. A spinner is divided into 3 equal areas and labeled 1, 2, and 3. The spinner is spun and an ordinary fair six-sided number die is rolled.

  a) Draw a possibility diagram to represent the possible outcomes.

  b) Find the probability of getting a number from the spinner that is greater than or equal to the number from the die.

Solve. Show your work.

20. A bag contains 5 balls labeled 1 to 5. A spinner is divided into 4 equal areas and labeled 1 to 4. One ball is selected and the spinner is spun. The sum of the two resulting numbers is noted.

    a) Draw a possibility diagram to represent the possible outcomes.

    b) Find the probability that the sum of the two resulting numbers is greater than 6.

21. Two fair six-sided number dice are rolled. The absolute value of the difference in the numbers rolled is noted.

    a) Draw a possibility diagram to represent the possible outcomes.

    b) Find the probability that the absolute value of the difference of the two resulting numbers is less than 2.

Solve. Show your work.

22. A bag contains 1 blue marble, 1 red marble and 2 yellow marbles. Dante randomly selects a marble from the bag, notes the color and places it back into the bag. He then randomly selects another marble and notes its color.

   a) Draw a tree diagram to represent the possible outcomes and the corresponding probabilities.

   b) What is the probability that the marbles selected are both red or both yellow?

23. A fruit basket contains 4 apples and 2 pears. Tom randomly selects a fruit to give to Maya. He then randomly selects another fruit to give to Harry.

   a) Draw a tree diagram to represent the possible outcomes and the corresponding probabilities.

   b) What is the probability that Tom gives Maya and Harry different types of fruits?

Name: _____   Date: _____

Solve. Show your work.

24. There are 3 teams in a dodge-ball competition: Team A, Team B, and Team C. Among a group of 25 boys, 7 of them support Team A, 8 of them support Team B, and the rest support Team C.

    a) A boy is randomly chosen from the group. Find the probability that he supports Team C.

    b) If 2 boys are randomly chosen from the group, what is the probability that they both support Team A or both support Team B?

25. In square *ABCD*, *M* and *N* are midpoints of $\overline{AB}$ and $\overline{AD}$.

    a) If a point is selected at random inside the square, calculate the probability that it is not inside △*MAN*.

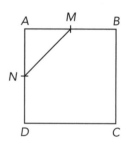

    b) If 2 points are selected at random inside the square, find the probability that one point is inside △*MAN* and the other is not.

Solve. Show your work.

26. There are 5 boys and 4 girls in a group. A child is randomly chosen.

    a)   What is the probability that the child is a boy?

    b)   If the first child chosen at random is a boy, what is the probability that the second child chosen is also a boy?

Name: _____   Date: _____

Solve. Show your work.

27. The probability that it rains is 0.6. Susan can choose to go out to play basketball, read a book at home, or go to sleep. If it does not rain, the probability that Susan goes out to play basketball is 0.5, reads a book at home is 0.3, and goes to sleep is 0.2. If it rains, the probability that Susan goes out to play basketball is 0.15, reads a book at home is 0.4, and goes to sleep is 0.45.

   a) Draw a tree diagram to represent the possible outcomes and their corresponding probabilities.

   b) Find the probability that Susan will read a book at home.

   c) Find the probability that it will not rain and Susan will go to sleep.

   d) Find the probability that Susan will go out to play basketball.

Solve. Show your work.

28. The data below shows the gender and favorite color of 12 students surveyed.

Gender	Male	Female	Male	Male	Female	Female
Favorite Color	Blue	Pink	Black	Blue	Blue	Green

Gender	Female	Female	Male	Male	Male	Male
Favorite Color	Pink	Black	Blue	Black	Green	Green

a) Construct a two-way table for the above data.

b) Describe the association between genders and favorite colors based on the given data.

Answers

Chapter 7

Lesson 7.1

1.

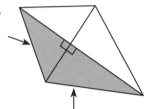

2.

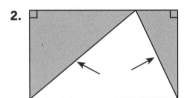

3. $x^2 = 24^2 + 7^2$
$x^2 = 576 + 49$
$x^2 = 625$
$x = \sqrt{625}$
$x = 25$

4. $x^2 = 10^2 + 7.5^2$
$x^2 = 100 + 56.25$
$x^2 = 156.25$
$x = \sqrt{156.25}$
$x = 12.5$

5. $26^2 = 10^2 + x^2$
$676 = 100 + x^2$
$676 - 100 = 100 + x^2 - 100$
$576 = x^2$
$x = \sqrt{576}$
$x = 24$

6. $41^2 = 40^2 + x^2$
$1{,}681 = 1{,}600 + x^2$
$1{,}681 - 1{,}600 = 1{,}600 + x^2 - 1{,}600$
$81 = x^2$
$x = \sqrt{81}$
$x = 9$

7. $11^2 = 8.8^2 + x^2$
$121 = 77.44 + x^2$
$121 - 77.44 = 77.44 + x^2 - 77.44$
$43.56 = x^2$
$x = \sqrt{43.56}$
$x = 6.6$
The value of x is 6.6.

$y^2 = x^2 + 10^2$
$y^2 = 43.56 + 100$
$y^2 = 143.56$
$y = \sqrt{143.56}$
$y \approx 12.0$
The value of y is approximately 12.0.

8. $11^2 = AD^2 + 8^2$
$121 = AD^2 + 64$
$121 - 64 = AD^2 + 64 - 64$
$57 = AD^2$
$AD = \sqrt{57}$
$AD \approx 7.55$
$12^2 = DC^2 + 8^2$
$144 = DC^2 + 64$
$144 - 64 = DC^2 + 64 - 64$
$80 = DC^2$
$DC = \sqrt{80}$
$DC \approx 8.94$
$x = 7.55 + 8.94$
$x = 16.49$
$x \approx 16.5$
The value of x is approximately 16.5.

9. $20^2 = 16^2 + x^2$
$400 = 256 + x^2$
$400 - 256 = 256 + x^2 - 256$
$144 = x^2$
$x = \sqrt{144}$
$x = 12$
The value of x is 12.
$y^2 = (16 + 4)^2 + 12^2$
$y^2 = 20^2 + 12^2$
$y^2 = 400 + 144$
$y^2 = 544$
$y = \sqrt{544}$
$y \approx 23.3$
The value of y is approximately 23.3.

10. $x^2 = 7^2 + 11^2$
$x^2 = 49 + 121$
$x^2 = 170$
$x = \sqrt{170}$
$x \approx 13.04$
The value of x is approximately 13.0.
$y^2 \approx 11^2 + (13.04 + 7)^2$
$y^2 = 11^2 + 20.04^2$
$y^2 \approx 121 + 401.60$
$y^2 = 522.60$
$y = \sqrt{522.60}$
$y \approx 22.9$
The value of y is approximately 22.9.

11. Field A:
$$36^2 + 48^2 \overset{?}{=} 60^2$$
$$1{,}296 + 2{,}304 \overset{?}{=} 3{,}600$$
$$3{,}600 = 3{,}600$$
So, Field A is a right triangle.
Field B:
$$40^2 + 50^2 \overset{?}{=} 60^2$$
$$1{,}600 + 2{,}500 \overset{?}{=} 3{,}600$$
$$4{,}100 \neq 3{,}600$$
So, Field B is not a right triangle.

12. Let the height of the wall be x feet.
$$10^2 = x^2 + 5^2$$
$$100 = x^2 + 25$$
$$100 - 25 = x^2 + 25 - 25$$
$$75 = x^2$$
$$x = \sqrt{75}$$
$$x \approx 8.7$$
The height of the wall is approximately 8.7 feet.

13. Let the length of the cable be x feet.
$$x^2 = 6^2 + 12^2$$
$$x^2 = 36 + 144$$
$$x^2 = 180$$
$$x = \sqrt{180}$$
$$x \approx 13.4$$
The length of the cable is approximately 13.4 feet.

14. Let the distance from the base of the escalator to the point on the first floor directly below the top of the escalator be x feet.
$$30^2 = 12^2 + x^2$$
$$900 = 144 + x^2$$
$$900 - 144 = 144 + x^2 - 144$$
$$756 = x^2$$
$$x = \sqrt{756}$$
$$x \approx 27.5$$
The distance from the base of the escalator to the point on the first floor directly below the top of the escalator is approximately 27.5 feet.

15. Let the vertical height of the balloon above the ground be x meters.
$$100^2 = 20^2 + x^2$$
$$10{,}000 = 400 + x^2$$
$$10{,}000 - 400 = 400 + x^2 - 400$$
$$9{,}600 = x^2$$
$$x = \sqrt{9{,}600}$$
$$x \approx 98.0$$
The vertical height of the balloon is approximately 98 meters above the ground.

16. Difference in height between Stations A and B
$$= 50 - 20$$
$$= 30 \text{ m}$$
$$\frac{1}{2} \text{ km} = 500 \text{ m}$$
Let the length of the cable be x meters.
$$x^2 = 500^2 + 30^2$$
$$x^2 = 250{,}000 + 900$$
$$x^2 = 250{,}900$$
$$x = \sqrt{250{,}900}$$
$$x \approx 500.9$$
The length of the cable is approximately 500.9 meters.

17. Let the longest line be x feet.
$$x^2 = 6^2 + 3^2$$
$$x^2 = 36 + 9$$
$$x^2 = 45$$
$$x = \sqrt{45}$$
$$x \approx 6.7$$
The longest line that can be drawn across the whiteboard is approximately 6.7 feet.

18. Let the length of the path be p meters.
$$p^2 = 30^2 + 20^2$$
$$p^2 = 900 + 400$$
$$p^2 = 1{,}300$$
$$p = \sqrt{1{,}300}$$
$$p \approx 36.1$$
Jill walked approximately 36.1 meters.
Difference between the two routes
$$\approx 50 - 36.1$$
$$= 13.9 \text{ m}$$
The difference in distance between the two routes is about 13.9 meters.

19. a) In $\triangle ABC$,
$$AB^2 = BE^2 + AE^2$$
$$AB^2 = 12^2 + 15^2$$
$$AB^2 = 144 + 225$$
$$AB^2 = 369$$
$$AB = \sqrt{369}$$
$$AB \approx 19.2 \text{ ft}$$
$$CD = AB$$
$$CD \approx 19.2 \text{ ft}$$
The length of the string is approximately 19.2 feet.

b) In $\triangle CED$,
$$CD^2 = CE^2 + DE^2$$
$$AB^2 = CE^2 + 13^2$$
$$369 = CE^2 + 169$$
$$369 - 169 = CE^2 + 169 - 169$$
$$200 = CE^2$$
$$CE = \sqrt{200}$$
$$CE \approx 14.1 \text{ ft}$$
$$AC = AE - CE$$
$$AC \approx 15 - 14.1$$
$$AC = 0.9 \text{ ft}$$
The difference between the points A and C is about 0.9 feet.

20. a) Let the side of the square be x inches.
$$28^2 = x^2 + x^2$$
$$784 = 2x^2$$
$$\frac{784}{2} = \frac{2x^2}{2}$$
$$392 = x^2$$
$$x = \sqrt{392}$$
$$x \approx 19.8$$
Perimeter of square $\approx 4 \cdot 19.8$
$$= 79.2 \text{ in.}$$
The perimeter of the square is about 79.2 inches.

b) Area of the square $= x \cdot x$
$$\approx 19.8 \cdot 19.8$$
$$= 392 \text{ in}^2$$
The area of the square is about 392 square inches.

21. a) In $\triangle ADB$,
$$34.4^2 = BD^2 + 22.6^2$$
$$1{,}183.36 = BD^2 + 510.76$$
$$1{,}183.36 - 510.76 = BD^2 + 510.76 - 510.76$$
$$672.6 = BD^2$$
$$BD = \sqrt{672.6}$$
$$BD \approx 25.93$$
$CD \approx 25.93 - 13$
$$= 12.93 \text{ in.}$$
In $\triangle ADC$,
$$AC^2 = 12.93^2 + 22.6^2$$
$$AC^2 \approx 677.94$$
$$AC = \sqrt{677.94}$$
$$AC \approx 26.0 \text{ in.}$$
The length of $\overline{AC}$ is approximately 26 inches.

b) Area of $\triangle ACD = \frac{1}{2} \cdot CD \cdot AD$
$$\approx \frac{1}{2} \cdot 12.93 \cdot 22.6$$
$$\approx 146.1 \text{ in}^2$$
The area of triangle ACD is approximately 146.1 square inches.

22. a)
$$AC^2 = 40^2 + 45^2$$
$$AC^2 = 3{,}625$$
$$AC = \sqrt{3{,}625}$$
$$AC \approx 60.2 \text{ m}$$
The length of $\overline{AC}$ is approximately 60.2 meters.

b) The length of $\overline{BP}$ is the perpendicular distance between B and $\overline{AC}$.
Area of $\triangle ABC$:
$$\frac{1}{2} \cdot AC \cdot BP = \frac{1}{2} \cdot BC \cdot AB$$
$$\frac{1}{2} \cdot 60.2 \cdot BP \approx \frac{1}{2} \cdot 45 \cdot 40$$
$$30.1 \cdot BP = 900$$
$$\frac{30.1 \cdot BP}{30.1} = \frac{900}{30.1}$$
$$BP \approx 29.9 \text{ m}$$
The length of $\overline{BP}$ is approximately 29.9 meters.

23. a) In $\triangle PQR$,
$$PR^2 = 80^2 + 65^2$$
$$PR^2 = 6{,}400 + 4{,}225$$
$$PR^2 = 10{,}625$$
$$PR = \sqrt{10{,}625}$$
$$PR \approx 103.1 \text{ ft}$$
In $\triangle PTS$,
$TS = 80 - 30$
$$= 50 \text{ ft}$$
$PT = QR$
$$= 65 \text{ ft}$$
$$PS^2 = 50^2 + 65^2$$
$$PS^2 = 2{,}500 + 4{,}225$$
$$PS^2 = 6{,}725$$
$$PS = \sqrt{6{,}725}$$
$$\approx 82.0 \text{ ft}$$
Perimeter of shaded triangle
$$\approx 103.1 + 82 + 30$$
$$= 215.1 \text{ ft}$$
The perimeter of the shaded triangle is approximately 215.1 feet.

b) Area of shaded triangle
$$= \frac{1}{2} \cdot SR \cdot PT$$
$$= \frac{1}{2} \cdot 30 \cdot 65$$
$$= 975 \text{ ft}^2$$
The area of the shaded triangle is 975 square feet.

c) Area of shaded triangle:

$$\frac{1}{2} \cdot PR \cdot SU = 975$$

$$\frac{1}{2} \cdot 103.1 \cdot SU \approx 975$$

$$\frac{51.55 \cdot SU}{51.55} = \frac{975}{51.55}$$

$$SU \approx 18.9 \text{ ft}$$

The length of $\overline{SU}$ is approximately 18.9 feet.

24. a) Let the distance between Town A and Town C on the map be x centimeters.

$$x^2 = 6^2 + 7^2$$
$$x^2 = 36 + 49$$
$$x^2 = 85$$

Let the distance between Town A and Town D on the map be y centimeters.

$$x^2 = 8^2 + y^2$$
$$85 = 64 + y^2$$
$$85 - 64 = 64 + y^2 - 64$$
$$21 = y^2$$
$$y = \sqrt{21}$$
$$y \approx 4.58 \text{ cm}$$

Let the actual distance between Town A and Town D be d kilometers.

Map scale:

1 : 50,000

50,000 cm = 0.5 km

$$\frac{1}{0.5} = \frac{4.58}{d}$$

$$0.5 \cdot \frac{1}{0.5} = \frac{4.58}{d} \cdot 0.5$$

$$1 = \frac{2.29}{d}$$

$$d \cdot 1 = \frac{2.29}{d} \cdot d$$

$$d \approx 2.3 \text{ km}$$

The actual distance between Town A and Town D is approximately 2.3 kilometers.

25. In $\triangle ABD$,

$$AB^2 + AD^2 \overset{?}{=} BD^2$$
$$20^2 + 16^2 \overset{?}{=} 25^2$$
$$656 \neq 625$$

So, triangle ABD is not a right triangle.

In $\triangle BCD$,

$$BD^2 + CD^2 \overset{?}{=} BC^2$$
$$25^2 + 60^2 \overset{?}{=} 65^2$$
$$4{,}225 = 4{,}225$$

So, triangle BCD is a right triangle.

Lesson 7.2

1. Plot a point $X(-4, -3)$ to form the third vertex of a right triangle.

$$PX = |3 - (-3)| = 6 \text{ units}$$
$$QX = |4 - (-4)| = 8 \text{ units}$$
$$PX^2 + QX^2 = PQ^2$$
$$6^2 + 8^2 = PQ^2$$
$$36 + 64 = PQ^2$$
$$100 = PQ^2$$
$$PQ = \sqrt{100}$$
$$PQ = 10$$

The exact distance between points P and Q is 10 units.

2. a) Distance from A to B

$$= \sqrt{(0 - 3)^2 + [-4 - (-2)]^2}$$
$$= \sqrt{(-3)^2 + (-2)^2}$$
$$= \sqrt{9 + 4}$$
$$= \sqrt{13}$$
$$\approx 3.6 \text{ units}$$

b) Distance from C to D

$$= \sqrt{(4 - 2)^2 + [2 - (-6)]^2}$$
$$= \sqrt{2^2 + 8^2}$$
$$= \sqrt{4 + 64}$$
$$= \sqrt{68}$$
$$\approx 8.2 \text{ units}$$

c) Distance from E to F

$$= \sqrt{[3 - (-7)]^2 + (-3 - 8)^2}$$
$$= \sqrt{10^2 + 11^2}$$
$$= \sqrt{100 + 121}$$
$$= \sqrt{221}$$
$$\approx 14.9 \text{ units}$$

d) Distance from G to H

$$= \sqrt{[-1 - (-2)]^2 + [-4 - (-5)]^2}$$
$$= \sqrt{1^2 + 1^2}$$
$$= \sqrt{1 + 1}$$
$$= \sqrt{2}$$
$$\approx 1.4 \text{ units}$$

Points G and H are closest to each other.

3. Distance from P to Q

$= \sqrt{[3 - (-3)]^2 + (3 - 4)^2}$

$= \sqrt{36 + 1}$

$= \sqrt{37}$ units

Distance from Q to R

$= \sqrt{(4 - 3)^2 + (-3 - 3)^2}$

$= \sqrt{1 + 36}$

$= \sqrt{37}$ units

Distance from P to R

$= \sqrt{[4 - (-3)]^2 + (-3 - 4)^2}$

$= \sqrt{49 + 49}$

$= \sqrt{98}$ units

The longest side is PR.

$PQ^2 + QR^2 \overset{?}{=} PR^2$

$(\sqrt{37})^2 + (\sqrt{37})^2 \overset{?}{=} (\sqrt{98})^2$

$74 \neq 98$

So, triangle PQR is not a right triangle.

4. **a)** Distance from Mary's home to the bank

$= \sqrt{[1 - (-5)]^2 + (2 - 4)^2}$

$= \sqrt{6^2 + (-2)^2}$

$= \sqrt{36 + 4}$

$= \sqrt{40}$

≈ 6.3 km

The bank is approximately 6.3 kilometers from Mary's home.

b) Distance from Mary's home to the cinema

$= \sqrt{[1 - (-1)]^2 + [2 - (-4)]^2}$

$= \sqrt{2^2 + 6^2}$

$= \sqrt{4 + 36}$

$= \sqrt{40}$

≈ 6.3 km

The cinema is approximately 6.3 kilometers from Mary's home.

c) Distance from Mary's home to the post office

$= \sqrt{(4 - 1)^2 + (3 - 2)^2}$

$= \sqrt{3^2 + (-1)^2}$

$= \sqrt{9 + 1}$

$= \sqrt{10}$

≈ 3.2 km

The post office is approximately 3.2 kilometers from Mary's home.

d) Distance from Mary's home to the school

$= \sqrt{(1 - 3)^2 + [2 - (-4)]^2}$

$= \sqrt{(-2)^2 + 6^2}$

$= \sqrt{4 + 36}$

$= \sqrt{40}$

≈ 6.3 km

The school is approximately 6.3 kilometers from Mary's home.

5. The bank, the cinema, and the school are the same distance from Mary's home.

6. Distance from school to the post office

$= \sqrt{(4 - 3)^2 + [3 - (-4)]^2}$

$= \sqrt{(-1)^2 + (7)^2}$

$= \sqrt{1 + 49}$

$= \sqrt{50}$

≈ 7.1 km

Total distance traveled

$\approx 6.3 + 7.1 + 3.2$

$= 16.6$ km

The total distance Mary traveled was approximately 16.6 kilometers.

7. a) $AP = \sqrt{(2-3)^2 + (3-1)^2}$

$= \sqrt{1+4}$

$= \sqrt{5}$ km

$PQ = \sqrt{(3-0)^2 + [1-(-2)]^2}$

$= \sqrt{9+9}$

$= \sqrt{18}$ km

$QB = 4$ km

Route via P and $Q = \sqrt{5} + \sqrt{18} + 4$

≈ 10.48 km

$AR = \sqrt{[2-(-3)]^2 + (3-4)^2}$

$= \sqrt{25+1}$

$= \sqrt{26}$ km

$RB = \sqrt{[-3-(-4)]^2 + [4-(-2)]^2}$

$= \sqrt{1+36}$

$= \sqrt{37}$ km

Route via $R = \sqrt{26} + \sqrt{37}$

≈ 11.18 km

The shorter route is the route that takes him through Towns P and Q.

b) Difference between the two routes

$\approx 11.18 - 10.48$

$= 0.7$ km

The difference in the distances of the two routes is 0.7 kilometers.

8. a) Distance from boat to lighthouse

$= \sqrt{[2-(-3)]^2 + [3-(-4)]^2}$

$= \sqrt{5^2 + 7^2}$

$= \sqrt{25+49}$

$= \sqrt{74}$ units

Actual distance from boat to lighthouse

$= \sqrt{74} \cdot \dfrac{1}{2}$

≈ 4.3 mi

The boat is approximately 4.3 miles from the lighthouse.

b) 20 min $= \dfrac{1}{3}$ h

Distance = Speed · Time

$4.3 \approx$ Speed $\cdot \dfrac{1}{3}$

$3 \cdot 4.3 =$ Speed $\cdot \dfrac{1}{3} \cdot 3$

Speed $= 12.9$ mi/h

The speed of the boat is 12.9 miles per hour.

Lesson 7.3

1. $a^2 = 12^2 + 5^2$

$a^2 = 144 + 25$

$a^2 = 169$

$a = \sqrt{169}$

$a = 13$

2. $\left(\dfrac{b}{2}\right)^2 + 24^2 = 25^2$

$\left(\dfrac{b}{2}\right)^2 + 576 = 625$

$\left(\dfrac{b}{2}\right)^2 + 576 - 576 = 625 - 576$

$\left(\dfrac{b}{2}\right)^2 = 49$

$\dfrac{b}{2} = \sqrt{49}$

$\dfrac{b}{2} = 7$

$2 \cdot \dfrac{b}{2} = 7 \cdot 2$

$b = 14$

3. Diameter of cylinder $= 5 \cdot 2$

$= 10$ cm

$x^2 = 30^2 + 10^2$

$x^2 = 900 + 100$

$x^2 = 1,000$

$x = \sqrt{1,000}$

$x \approx 31.6$

4. Radius of sphere $= \dfrac{1}{2} \cdot 1.2$

$= 0.6$ m

$y^2 = 0.6^2 + 0.6^2$

$y^2 = 0.36 + 0.36$

$y^2 = 0.72$

$y = \sqrt{0.72}$

$y \approx 0.8$

5. Let the side of the square base be x inches.

$$\left(\frac{x}{2}\right)^2 + 24^2 = 26^2$$

$$\left(\frac{x}{2}\right)^2 + 576 = 676$$

$$\left(\frac{x}{2}\right)^2 + 576 - 576 = 676 - 576$$

$$\left(\frac{x}{2}\right)^2 = 100$$

$$\frac{x}{2} = \sqrt{100}$$

$$\frac{x}{2} = 10$$

$$2 \cdot \frac{x}{2} = 10 \cdot 2$$

$$x = 20$$

Surface area of the pyramid
$$= 20 \cdot 20 + 4 \cdot \frac{1}{2} \cdot 20 \cdot 24$$
$$= 400 + 960$$
$$= 1{,}360 \text{ in}^2$$
The total surface area of the pyramid is 1,360 square inches.

6. Radius of cone $= \frac{1}{2} \cdot 20$

$$= 10 \text{ cm}$$

Let the slant height of the cone be x centimeters.
$x^2 = 50^2 + 10^2$
$x^2 = 2{,}500 + 100$
$x^2 = 2{,}600$
$x = \sqrt{2{,}600}$
$x \approx 50.99$
Curved surface area of cone
$= \pi \cdot r \cdot x$
$\approx 3.14 \cdot 10 \cdot 50.99$
$\approx 1{,}601.1 \text{ cm}^2$
The surface area Helen has to paint is approximately 1,601.1 square centimeters.

7. Radius of cone $= \frac{1}{2} \cdot 50$

$$= 25$$

Let the slant height of the cone be s inches.
$s^2 = 25^2 + 40^2$
$s^2 = 625 + 1{,}600$
$s^2 = 2{,}225$
$s = \sqrt{2{,}225}$
$s \approx 47.2$
The slant height of the cone is approximately 47.2 inches.

8. a) $AM^2 = AD^2 + DM^2$
$AM^2 = 20^2 + 15^2$
$AM^2 = 400 + 225$
$AM^2 = 625$
$AM = \sqrt{625}$
$AM = 25 \text{ cm}$
The distance from point A to point M is 25 centimeters.

b) The shortest distance between the fly's initial position and the spider's initial position is represented by AN.
$AN^2 = AM^2 + MN^2$
$AN^2 = 25^2 + 15^2$
$AN^2 = 625 + 225$
$AN^2 = 850$
$AN = \sqrt{850}$
$AN \approx 29.2 \text{ cm}$
The shortest distance between the fly's initial position and the spider's initial position is approximately 29.2 centimeters.

9. Radius of cone $= \frac{1}{2} \cdot 3$

$$= 1.5 \text{ ft}$$

Let the height of the cone be x feet.
$x^2 + 1.5^2 = 3^2$
$x^2 + 2.25 = 9$
$x^2 + 2.25 - 2.25 = 9 - 2.25$
$x^2 = 6.75$
$x = \sqrt{6.75}$
$x \approx 2.6$
Height of composite solid
$\approx 2 \cdot 2.6$
$= 5.2 \text{ ft}$
The height of the composite solid is approximately 5.2 feet.

10. Let the radius of the cone be r inches.
$r^2 + 9^2 = 10^2$
$r^2 + 81 = 100$
$r^2 + 81 - 81 = 100 - 81$
$r^2 = 19$
$r = \sqrt{19}$
$r \approx 4.359$
Circumference of base of cone
$= 2 \cdot \pi \cdot r$
$\approx 2 \cdot 3.14 \cdot 4.359$
$\approx 27.4 \text{ in.}$
Perimeter of Figure B
$\approx 10 + 10 + 27.4$
$= 47.4 \text{ in.}$
The perimeter of Figure B is approximately 47.4 inches.

11. a) Let the length of the diagonal of the base be x meters.

$$\left(\frac{x}{2}\right)^2 + 4.5^2 = 5^2$$

$$\left(\frac{x}{2}\right)^2 + 20.25 = 25$$

$$\left(\frac{x}{2}\right)^2 + 20.25 - 20.25 = 25 - 20.25$$

$$\left(\frac{x}{2}\right)^2 = 4.75$$

$$\frac{x}{2} = \sqrt{4.75}$$

$$\frac{x}{2} \approx 2.179$$

$$2 \cdot \frac{x}{2} = 2 \cdot 2.179$$

$$x = 4.358$$

The length of the diagonal of the base is 4.358 meters.

b) Let the side of the square base be y meters.
So, the area of the square is y^2 square meters.

$$y^2 + y^2 = x^2$$

$$2y^2 \approx 4.358^2$$

$$2y^2 \approx 18.99$$

$$\frac{2y^2}{2} \approx \frac{18.99}{2}$$

$$y^2 \approx 9.5$$

The area of the base of the pyramid is approximately 9.5 square meters.

Lesson 7.4

1. a) Let the unknown side of the base of the triangular prism be x inches.

$$x^2 + 20^2 = 25^2$$

$$x^2 + 400 = 625$$

$$x^2 + 400 - 400 = 625 - 400$$

$$x^2 = 225$$

$$x = \sqrt{225}$$

$$x = 15$$

Volume of prism

$$= \frac{1}{2} \cdot 15 \cdot 20 \cdot 14$$

$$= 2,100 \text{ in}^3$$

Volume of cylinder

$$\approx 3.14 \cdot 3.5^2 \cdot 14$$

$$\approx 538.5 \text{ in}^3$$

Volume of composite solid

$$\approx 538.5 + 2,100$$

$$= 2,638.5 \text{ in}^3$$

The volume of the composite solid is approximately 2,638.5 cubic inches.

b) Let the height of the cone be x feet.
Radius of cone = 1 ft

$$x^2 + 1^2 = 4^2$$

$$x^2 + 1 = 16$$

$$x^2 + 1 - 1 = 16 - 1$$

$$x^2 = 15$$

$$x = \sqrt{15}$$

$$x \approx 3.87$$

Volume of cone

$$\approx \frac{1}{3} \cdot 3.14 \cdot 1^2 \cdot 3.87$$

$$\approx 4.1 \text{ ft}^3$$

Volume of cylinder

$$\approx 3.14 \cdot 1^2 \cdot 5$$

$$= 15.7 \text{ ft}^3$$

Volume of composite solid

$$\approx 15.7 + 4.1$$

$$= 19.8 \text{ ft}^3$$

The volume of the composite solid is approximately 19.8 cubic feet.

2. Let the radius of the hemisphere be x inches.

$$x^2 + x^2 = 10^2$$

$$2x^2 = 100$$

$$\frac{2x^2}{2} = \frac{100}{2}$$

$$x^2 = 50$$

$$x = \sqrt{50}$$

$$x \approx 7.07$$

Volume of hemisphere

$$\approx \frac{1}{2} \cdot \frac{4}{3} \cdot 3.14 \cdot 7.07^3$$

$$\approx 739.77 \text{ in}^3$$

Radius of cylinder

$$\approx 7.07 + 3$$

$$= 10.07 \text{ in.}$$

Volume of cylinder

$$\approx 3.14 \cdot 10.07^2 \cdot 12$$

$$\approx 3,820.94 \text{ in}^3$$

Volume of solid

$$= 3,820.94 - 739.77$$

$$= 3,081.2 \text{ in}^3$$

The volume of the solid is approximately 3,081.2 cubic inches.

3. Radius of cone = 10 cm

a) Let the height of the cone be x centimeters.

$$26^2 = 10^2 + x^2$$

$$676 = 100 + x^2$$

$$676 - 100 = 100 + x^2 - 100$$

$$x^2 = 576$$

$$x = \sqrt{576}$$

$$x = 24$$

The height of the cone is 24 centimeters.

b) Volume of cone $\approx \frac{1}{3} \cdot 3.14 \cdot 10^2 \cdot 24$

$ = 2{,}512 \text{ cm}^3$

Volume of hemisphere $\approx \frac{1}{2} \cdot \frac{4}{3} \cdot 3.14 \cdot 10^3$

$ \approx 2{,}093.3 \text{ cm}^3$

Volume of solid $\approx 2{,}093.3 + 2{,}512$

$ = 4{,}605.3 \text{ cm}^3$

The volume of the solid is approximately 4,605.3 cubic centimeters.

4. a) Let the length of the diagonal be x inches.

$x^2 = 12^2 + 12^2$

$x^2 = 288$

$x = \sqrt{288}$

$x \approx 17.0$

The length of the diagonal of the base is approximately 17.0 inches.

b) Length of half the diagonal $= \frac{1}{2} \cdot \sqrt{288}$

$ \approx 8.485 \text{ in.}$

Let the height of the pyramid be y inches.

$y^2 + 8.485^2 \approx 10^2$

$y^2 + 8.485^2 - 8.485^2 = 10^2 - 8.485^2$

$y^2 = 28.00$

$y = \sqrt{28}$

$y \approx 5.3$

The height of the pyramid is approximately 5.3 inches.

c) Volume of pyramid $= \frac{1}{3} \cdot 12 \cdot 12 \cdot \sqrt{28}$

$ \approx 254.0 \text{ in}^3$

Volume of rectangular block $= 12 \cdot 12 \cdot 8$

$ = 1{,}152 \text{ in}^3$

Total volume $\approx 1{,}152 + 254.0$

$ = 1{,}406.0 \text{ in}^3$

The volume of the solid is approximately 1,406 cubic inches.

5. a) Radius of cone $= 6$ cm

Let the depth of the hole be x centimeters.

$x^2 + 6^2 = 10^2$

$x^2 + 36 = 100$

$x^2 + 36 - 36 = 100 - 36$

$x^2 = 64$

$x = \sqrt{64}$

$x = 8$

The depth of the cone is 8 centimeters.

b) Volume of cylinder

$\approx 3.14 \cdot 6^2 \cdot 18$

$= 2{,}034.72 \text{ cm}^3$

Volume of cone-shaped hole

$\approx \frac{1}{3} \cdot 3.14 \cdot 6^2 \cdot 8$

$= 301.44 \text{ cm}^3$

Volume of remaining metal

$= 2{,}034.72 - 301.44$

$\approx 1{,}777.7 \text{ cm}^3$

The volume of the remaining metal is approximately 1,777.7 cubic centimeters.

6. a) Let the diameter of the base of the cone be x inches.

$x^2 = 5^2 + 5^2$

$x^2 = 50$

$x = \sqrt{50}$

$x \approx 7.071$

Radius of hemisphere

$=$ Radius of base of cone

$\approx \frac{1}{2} \cdot 7.071$

$= 3.5355 \text{ in.}$

The radius of the hemisphere is approximately 3.5 inches.

b) Let the height of the cone be y inches.

$y^2 + 3.5355^2 = 5^2$

$y^2 + 3.5355^2 - 3.5355^2 = 5^2 - 3.5355^2$

$y^2 \approx 12.50$

$y = \sqrt{12.50}$

$y \approx 3.536$

Volume of cone $\approx \frac{1}{3} \cdot 3.14 \cdot 3.5355^2 \cdot 3.536$

$\approx 46.26 \text{ in}^3$

Volume of cylinder $\approx 3.14 \cdot 3.5355^2 \cdot 25$

$\approx 981.23 \text{ in}^3$

Volume of hemisphere

$\approx \frac{1}{2} \cdot \frac{4}{3} \cdot 3.14 \cdot 3.5355^3$

$\approx 92.51 \text{ in}^3$

Volume of model

$\approx 46.26 + 981.23 + 92.51$

$\approx 1{,}120.0 \text{ in}^3$

The volume of the solid is approximately 1,120 cubic inches.

7. a) Let the diagonal of the pyramid base be x inches.

$x^2 = 10^2 + 10^2$

$x^2 = 100 + 100$

$x^2 = 200$

$x = \sqrt{200}$

$x \approx 14.14$

Length of half the diagonal $\approx \frac{1}{2} \cdot 14.14$

$= 7.07$ in.

Let the height of the pyramid be y inches.

$y^2 + 7.07^2 = 10^2$

$y^2 + 7.07^2 - 7.07^2 = 10^2 - 7.07^2$

$y^2 = 50.02$

$y = \sqrt{50.02}$

$y \approx 7.1$

The height of the pyramid is approximately 7.1 inches.

b) Volume of pyramid $\approx \frac{1}{3} \cdot 10^2 \cdot \sqrt{50.02}$

$= 235.75$ in^3

Let the height of the base of the prism be z inches.

$z^2 = 10^2 - 5^2$

$z^2 = 100 - 25$

$z^2 = 75$

$z = \sqrt{75}$

$z \approx 8.66$

Volume of prism $\approx \frac{1}{2} \cdot 10 \cdot 8.66 \cdot 10$

$= 433$ in^3

Volume of solid $\approx 433 + 235.75$

≈ 668.8 in^3

The volume of the solid is approximately 668.8 cubic inches.

8. Let the height of the triangular face of the triangular prism be x inches.

$x^2 + 0.6^2 = 1^2$

$x^2 + 0.36 = 1$

$x^2 + 0.36 - 0.36 = 1 - 0.36$

$x^2 = 0.64$

$x = \sqrt{0.64}$

$x = 0.8$

Volume of triangular prism

$= \frac{1}{2} \cdot 1.2 \cdot 0.8 \cdot 8$

$= 3.84$ in^3

Volume of rectangular prism

$= 8 \cdot 1.2 \cdot 0.6$

$= 5.76$ in^3

Volume of solid

$= 3.84 + 5.76$

$= 9.6$ in^3

The volume of the entire wooden nameplate is 9.6 cubic inches.

Brain @ Work

1. a) Distance from C to P

$= \sqrt{(8-4)^2 + (-10-2)^2}$

$= \sqrt{4^2 + (-12)^2}$

$= \sqrt{160}$ units

Distance from C to Q

$= \sqrt{(6-4)^2 + (8-2)^2}$

$= \sqrt{2^2 + 6^2}$

$= \sqrt{40}$ units

Distance from C to R

$= \sqrt{[4-(-8)]^2 + (2-6)^2}$

$= \sqrt{12^2 + (-4)^2}$

$= \sqrt{160}$ units

Distance from C to S

$= \sqrt{[4-(-8)]^2 + [2-(-2)]^2}$

$= \sqrt{12^2 + 4^2}$

$= \sqrt{160}$ units

Three points P (8, −10), R (−8, 6), and S (−8, −2) are the same distance from point C. The distance of point Q (6, 8) from point C does not lie the same as the rest. Therefore, point Q does not lie on the circumference of the circle.

b) The radius of the circle is $\sqrt{160}$ units. Since point Q is at a distance of $\sqrt{40}$ units from point C which is less than the radius ($\sqrt{160}$ units), point Q lies inside the circle.

2. Surface area of bigger cylinder

$\approx 2 \cdot 3.14 \cdot 5 \cdot 6 + 3.14 \cdot 5^2$

$= 188.4 + 78.5$

$= 266.9$ in^2

Curved surface area of smaller cylinder

$\approx 2 \cdot 3.14 \cdot 3 \cdot 6$

$= 113.04$ in^2

Height of entire cone

$= 4.5 + 6.5$

$= 11$ in.

Let the slant height of the entire cone be y inches.

$y^2 = 11^2 + 5^2$

$y^2 = 146$

$y = \sqrt{146}$

$y \approx 12.08$

Curved surface area of entire cone

$\approx 3.14 \cdot 5 \cdot 12.08$

$= 189.66$ in^2

Surface area of model
= 266.9 + 113.04 + 189.66
= 569.6 in²
The approximate surface area of the model is
569.6 square inches.

Chapter 8

Lesson 8.1

1. Coordinates of image: $(-2 + 7, 5) = (5, 5)$

2. Coordinates of image: $(3 - 2, -7 - 8)$
$= (1, -15)$

3. Coordinates of image: $(8 + 6, -4 + 7)$
$= (14, 3)$

4.

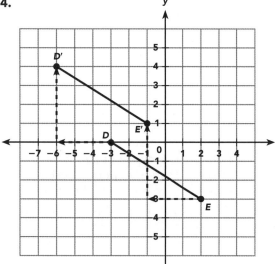

5.

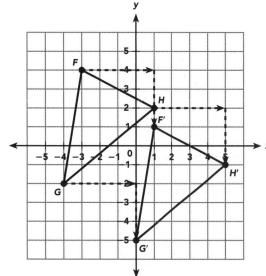

6.

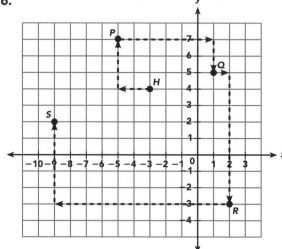

a) $P(-5, 7)$

b) $Q(1, 5)$

c) $R(2, -3)$

d) $S(-9, 2)$

7.

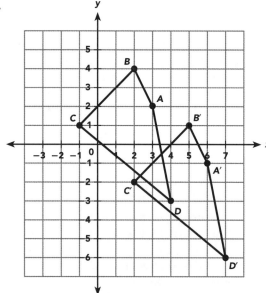

$A(3, 2)$ is translated to $A'(6, 1)$
Translation: 3 units to the right and 3 units
down.
Position of B' is $(2 + 3, 4 - 3) = (5, 1)$
Position of C' is $(-1 + 3, 1 - 3) = (2, -2)$
Position of D' is $(4 + 3, -3 - 3) = (7, -6)$

8.

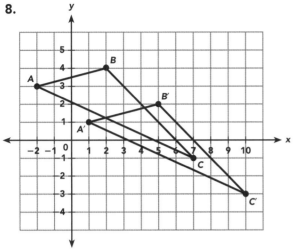

Translation moves each point (x, y) to $(x + 3, y − 2)$.

Original Point	Is Mapped Onto
$A (−2, 3)$	A' $(1, 1)$
$B (2, 4)$	B' $(5, 2)$
$C (7, −1)$	C' $(10, −3)$

9. Since A is moved under the translation 5 units to the left and 3 units up to A', A' can be moved back to A under the translation 5 units to the right and 3 units down to A.

Original Point	Is Mapped Onto
$A (12, 0)$	A' $(7, 3)$
$B (7, −2)$	B' $(2, 1)$

10.
$$y − 7 = x − 3 + 2$$
$$y − 7 = x − 1$$
$$y − 7 + 7 = x − 1 + 7$$
$$y = x + 6$$

The equation of the new line is $y = x + 6$. They both have a slope of 1.

11. 7 units to the right, 4 units down; (x, y) is mapped onto $(x + 7, y − 4)$.

Lesson 8.2

1.

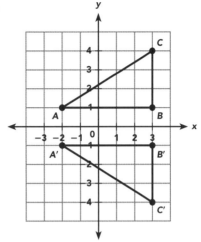

2.

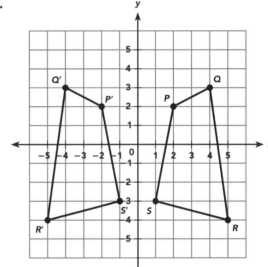

3.

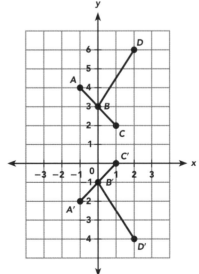

4.

Locations	Reflection in the y-axis	Reflection in the x-axis
A (−1, 3)	A′ (1, 3)	A″ (1, −3)
B (−3, 1)	B′ (3, 1)	B″ (3, −1)
C (−6, 1)	C′ (6, 1)	C″ (6, −1)
D (−6, 4)	D′ (6, 4)	D″ (6, −4)

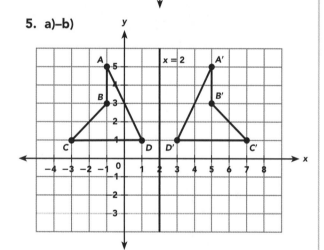

5. a)–b)

The coordinates are A′ (5, 5), B′ (5, 3), C′ (7, 1), and D′ (3, 1).

6. a)

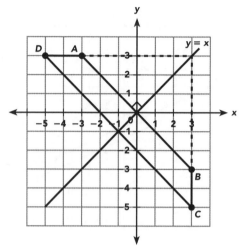

b) The equation of line of symmetry is y = x.

c) The coordinates of D is (−5, 3).

7. a)

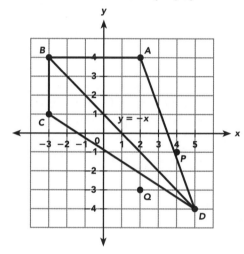

b) y = −x

c) Q (2, −3)

8. a) Q (0, 5)

b) R (5, 4)

c)

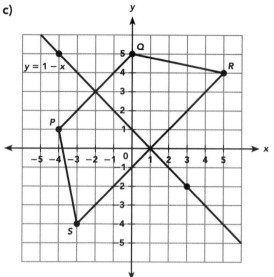

PQRS is a trapezoid with PQ ‖ SR.

Lesson 8.3

1. a) 90°

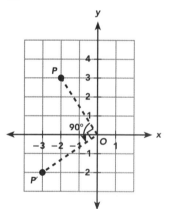

b) 270°

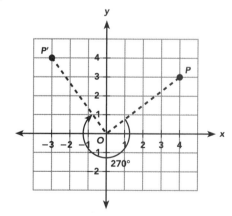

2. a) 90° clockwise

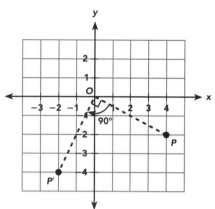

b) 180° clockwise or 180° counterclockwise

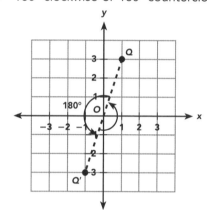

3.

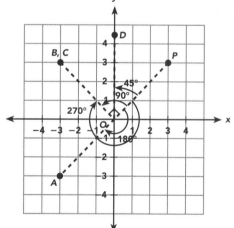

4.

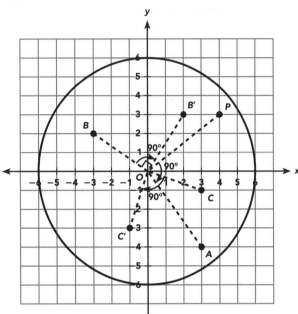

a) 90° clockwise about O

b) B′ (2, 3)

c) C (3, −1)

5.

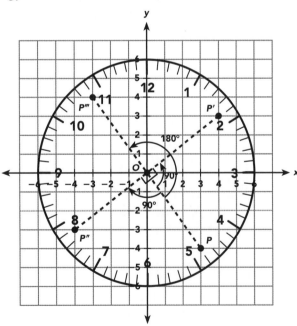

a) P′ (4, 3)

b) P″ (−4, −3)

c) P‴ (−3, 4)

6. a), c)

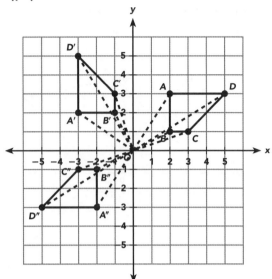

b) A′ (−3, 2), B′ (−1, 2), C′ (−1, 3), D′ (−3, 5)

d) A″ (−2, −3), B″ (−2, −1), C″ (−3, −1), D″ (−5, −3)

e) A″B″C″D″ is the image when A′B′C′D′ is rotated 90° counterclockwise about the origin. Or, A′B′C′D′ is the image when A″B″C″D″ is rotated 90° clockwise about the origin.

7. m∠AOB = $\frac{360°}{5}$ = 72°

The pentagon is rotated 72° clockwise about O or 288° counterclockwise about O.

8.

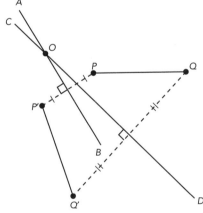

Join P to P′: Draw the ⊥ bisector AB of line joining P and P′.
Join Q to Q′: Draw the ⊥ bisector CD of line joining Q and Q′.
Mark O, the point where the two ⊥ bisectors cut. O is then the centre of rotation since OP = OP′ and OQ = OQ′.
Measure ∠POP′ and ∠QOQ′ and verify that they are equal. This angle is the angle of rotation.

Lesson 8.4

1. △POQ is a dilation of △AOB as they have a center of dilation O with scale factor 2.

2. △COD and △UOV are not dilations of each other as they do not share a center of dilation.

3. a) The lengths of the sides of the dilated copy are $3 \cdot 3 = 9$ in., $4 \cdot 3 = 12$ in., and $5 \cdot 3 = 15$ in.
The copy is an enlargement of the original triangle.

b) The lengths of the sides of the dilated copy are $3 \cdot \frac{1}{2} = 1\frac{1}{2}$ in., $4 \cdot \frac{1}{2} = 2$ in., and $5 \cdot \frac{1}{2} = 2\frac{1}{2}$ in.
The copy is a reduction of the original triangle.

c) The lengths of the sides of the dilated copy are $3 \cdot 1.2 = 3.6$ in., $4 \cdot 1.2 = 4.8$ in., and $5 \cdot 1.2 = 6$ in.
The copy is an enlargement of the original triangle.

d) The lengths of the sides of the dilated copy are $3 \cdot 80\% = 2.4$ in., $4 \cdot 80\% = 3.2$ in., and $5 \cdot 80\% = 4$ in.
The copy is a reduction of the original triangle.

4. a)

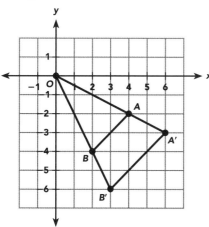

The image of the figure is △A′OB′.

b)

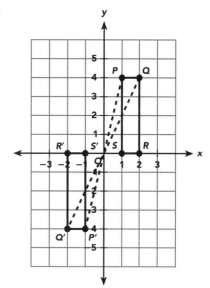

The image of the figure is rectangle P′Q′R′S′.

5. a)

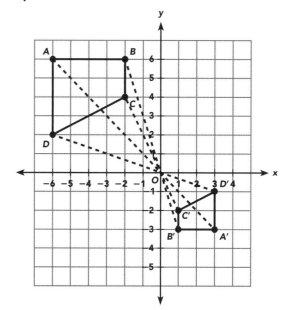

The image of the figure is A′B′C′D′.

b)

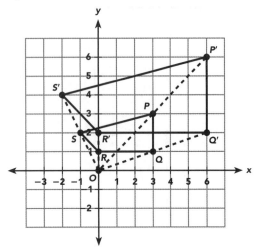

The image of the figure is rectangle
$P'Q'R'S'$.

6.

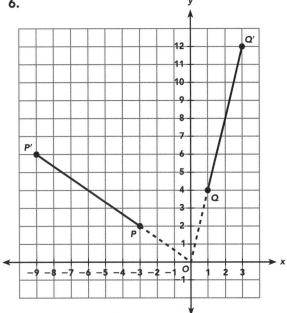

a) $OP = \sqrt{2^2 + 3^2}$

$= \sqrt{13}$

$OP' = \sqrt{9^2 + 6^2}$

$= \sqrt{117}$

Scale factor $= \dfrac{OP'}{OP}$

$= \dfrac{\sqrt{117}}{\sqrt{13}}$

$= \sqrt{\dfrac{117}{13}}$

$= \sqrt{9}$

$= 3$

b) $Q\,(1, 4)$

7.

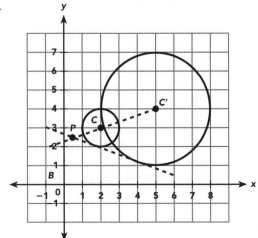

a) Scale factor $= \dfrac{\text{Radius of image circle}}{\text{Radius of original circle}}$

$= \dfrac{3}{1}$

$= 3$

b) $P\left(\dfrac{1}{2}, 2\dfrac{1}{2}\right)$

8. a), e)

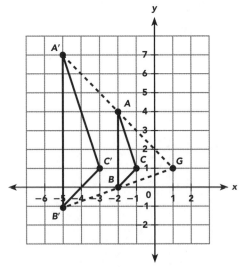

b) A is joined to A' and B is joined to B'.
Both lines intersect at the center of
dilation which is at $G\,(1, 1)$.

c)
$$GB = \sqrt{1^2 + 3^2}$$
$$= \sqrt{10}$$
$$GB' = \sqrt{2^2 + 6^2}$$
$$= \sqrt{40}$$

Scale factor $= \dfrac{GB'}{GB}$

$$= \dfrac{\sqrt{40}}{\sqrt{10}}$$

$$= \sqrt{\dfrac{40}{10}}$$

$$= \sqrt{4}$$

$$= 2$$

d) $h = -3$, $k = 1$

9. a), e)

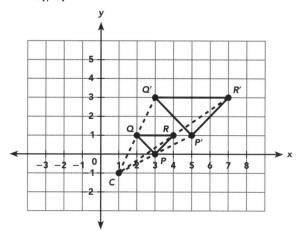

b) Q is joined to Q' and P is joined to P'. Both lines intersect at the center of dilation which is at $C\,(1, -1)$.

c)
$$CQ = \sqrt{2^2 + 1^2}$$
$$= \sqrt{5}$$

$$CQ' = \sqrt{4^2 + 2^2}$$
$$= \sqrt{20}$$

Scale factor $= \dfrac{CQ'}{CQ}$

$$= \dfrac{\sqrt{20}}{\sqrt{5}}$$

$$= \sqrt{\dfrac{20}{5}}$$

$$= \sqrt{4}$$

$$= 2$$

d) $h = 4$, $k = 1$

10. a), b)

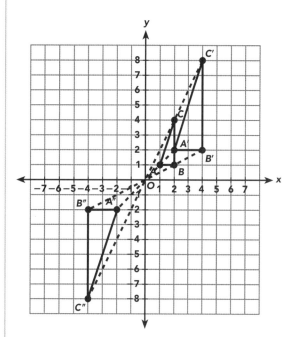

c) First transformation: dilation of scale factor -1 about O.
Second transformation: rotation of 180° (clockwise or counterclockwise) about O.

Lesson 8.5

1. a), b), c), d)

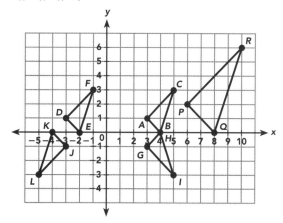

e) Transformations **a), b), c)**

f) Transformation **d)**

2. a), b)

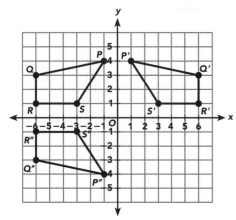

c) Dilation of scale factor −1 about O; Rotation of 180° (clockwise or counterclockwise) about O.

3. a) Translation of 10 units to the left; Reflection about the line $x = -1$

b) The line passing through the corresponding vertices of triangles Q and R, intersect at the point (2, 3). So, the center of dilation is (2, 0).

$$\text{Scale factor} = \frac{4}{2}$$
$$= 2$$

Triangle Q is mapped onto triangle R by a dilation with center at (2, 0) and scale factor 2.

4. a) It is a reflection about the line $y = x$.

b) It is a rotation of 90° counterclockwise about (1, 0).

c) It is a reflection about the y-axis.

d) It is a dilation of scale factor −2 about the center (2, 3).

5. a)

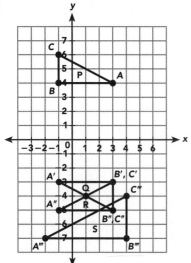

b) First transformation: Rotation of 180° (clockwise or counterclockwise) about
$$\left(1, \frac{1}{2}\right)$$

Second transformation: Dilation of scale factor −1 about $\left(1, \frac{1}{2}\right)$

c) It is a reflection about the line $y = -4$.

d) The line passing through the corresponding vertices of triangles R and S, intersect at the point (1, −1). So, the center of dilation is (1, −1).

$$\text{Scale factor} = \frac{6}{4}$$
$$= \frac{3}{2}$$

Triangle R is mapped onto triangle S by a dilation with center at (1, −1) and scale factor $\frac{3}{2}$.

6. a) There is no translation that maps the rhombus onto itself.

b) Reflection about the diagonal AC;
Reflection about the diagonal BD.

c) Rotation of 180° (clockwise or counterclockwise about the center of the rhombus (the center is the point where the diagonals cut);
Rotation of 360° (clockwise or counterclockwise) about the center of the rhombus.

d) Dilation of scale factor 1 or −1 with the center of the rhombus as the center of dilation.

Brain @ Work

1.

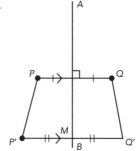

(1) Draw the ⊥ bisector of PQ and label it AB. AB is then the line of reflection.

(2) Draw a line through P′ perpendicular to PQ to cut AB at M. On this line, mark the point Q′ with MQ′ = MP′. Q′ is then the image of Q in the line of reflection.

2.

	Transformation
D is mapped onto C	Rotation of 90° counterclockwise about the origin
C is mapped onto B	Reflection about the y-axis
B is mapped onto A	Translation of 8 units to the left

Chapter 9

Lesson 9.1

1. $\triangle ABM$ is congruent to $\triangle ACM$.

   $\overline{AB}$ and $\overline{AC}$; $\overline{AM}$ and $\overline{AM}$; $\overline{BM}$ and $\overline{CM}$
   $\angle ABM$ and $\angle ACM$; $\angle AMB$ and $\angle AMC$;
   $\angle BAM$ and $\angle CAM$

2. $ADQP$ is congruent to $CBPQ$.

   $\overline{AD}$ and $\overline{CB}$; $\overline{DQ}$ and $\overline{BP}$; $\overline{QP}$ and $\overline{PQ}$;
   $\overline{AP}$ and $\overline{CQ}$
   $\angle PAD$ and $\angle QCB$; $\angle ADQ$ and $\angle CBP$;
   $\angle DQP$ and $\angle BPQ$; $\angle APQ$ and $\angle CQP$

3. 1st pair:
   $\triangle ABC$ is congruent to $\triangle ADC$.

   $\overline{AB}$ and $\overline{AD}$; $\overline{AC}$ and $\overline{AC}$; $\overline{BC}$ and $\overline{DC}$
   $\angle CAB$ and $\angle CAD$; $\angle ABC$ and $\angle ADC$;
   $\angle ACB$ and $\angle ACD$

   2nd pair:
   $\triangle ABP$ is congruent to $\triangle ADP$.

   $\overline{AB}$ and $\overline{AD}$; $\overline{AP}$ and $\overline{AP}$; $\overline{BP}$ and $\overline{DP}$
   $\angle PAB$ and $\angle PAD$; $\angle ABP$ and $\angle ADP$;
   $\angle APB$ and $\angle APD$

   3rd pair:
   $\triangle CBP$ is congruent to $\triangle CDP$.
   $\overline{CB}$ and $\overline{CD}$; $\overline{BP}$ and $\overline{DP}$; $\overline{CP}$ and $\overline{CP}$
   $\angle CBP$ and $\angle CDP$; $\angle CPB$ and $\angle CPD$;
   $\angle BCP$ and $\angle DCP$

4. In $\triangle PAB$ and $\triangle PCD$,

   $AB = CD$ [opposite sides of rhombus]
   $PA = PC$ [diagonals of rhombus bisect each other]
   $PB = PD$ [diagonals of rhombus bisect each other]
   By the SSS test, $\triangle PAB \cong \triangle PCD$.

5. **a)** 1st pair: $\triangle ABC \cong \triangle AFE$

   $AB = AF$ [sides of regular polygon]
   $BC = FE$ [sides of regular polygon]
   $AC = AE$ [given]
   By the SSS test, $\triangle ABC \cong \triangle AFE$.
   2nd pair: $\triangle ACD \cong \triangle AED$
   $AC = AE$ [given]

$CD = ED$ [sides of regular polygon]
$AD = AD$ [common side]
By the SSS test, $\triangle ACD \cong \triangle AED$.

b) $ABCD \cong AFED$

6. Since $\triangle ABC \cong \triangle DEC$, $m\angle ACB = m\angle DCE = u°$

$$u° + u° = 180° \text{ [Adj. } \angle s \text{ on a st. line]}$$
$$2u = 180$$
$$\frac{2u}{2} = \frac{180}{2}$$
$$u = 90$$

$m\angle DEC = m\angle ABC = 67.4°$
$v° = 180° - 90° - 67.4°$ [$\angle$sum of triangle]
$v = 22.6$
$w° = 180° - 67.4°$ [Adj. $\angle$s on a st. line]
$w = 112.6$
$AB = DE$
$x = 26$
$CE = CB = 10$ cm
In $\triangle DCE$, $y^2 + 10^2 = 26^2$

$$y^2 + 10^2 - 10^2 = 26^2 - 10^2$$
$$y^2 = 26^2 - 10^2$$
$$y = \sqrt{26^2 - 10^2}$$
$$y = 24$$

$$AC = DC$$
$$z + 10 = 24$$
$$z + 10 - 10 = 24 - 10$$
$$z = 14$$
$$z = 14$$

So, $u = 90$, $v = 22.6$, $w = 112.6$,
$x = 26$, $y = 24$, and $z = 14$.

7. In $\triangle PQR$ and $\triangle EAB$,
$m\angle PQR = m\angle EAB$

$$u = 69$$

$m\angle EBA = m\angle PRQ$

$$v° = 180° - m\angle PQR - m\angle RPQ$$
$$[\angle\text{sum of } \triangle]$$
$$v = 60$$

In $RSTP$ and $BCDE$, $(w - 2)$ cm $= ST$

$$ST = CD$$
$$w - 2 = 20$$
$$w - 2 + 2 = 20 + 2$$
$$w = 22$$
$$BC = RS$$
$$6x + 2y = 18$$
$$\frac{6x + 2y}{2} = \frac{18}{2}$$
$$3x + y = 9 \qquad\qquad \text{— Eq. 1}$$
$$PT = ED$$
$$8x + 3y = 25 \qquad\qquad \text{— Eq. 2}$$

Multiply Eq. 1 by 3:

$9x + 3y = 27$ — Eq. 3

Subtract Eq. 2 from Eq. 3:

$x = 2$

Substitute 2 for x into Eq. 1:

$3(2) + y = 9$

$6 + y = 9$

$6 + y - 6 = 9 - 6$

$y = 3$

8. a) In $\triangle ABC$ and $\triangle DEF$,

$m\angle ACB = m\angle DFE = 90°$ [given]

$AB = DE$ [opposite sides of parallelogram]

$AC = DF$ [⊥ distance between ll sides]

By the RHS test, $\triangle ABC \cong \triangle DEF$.

b) $DEAC \cong ABDF$

c) $DE = AB = 5$ ft

$EA = BD = 3 + 4$

$= 7$ ft

$AC^2 = AB^2 - BC^2$

$AC^2 = 5^2 - 3^2$

$AC = \sqrt{5^2 - 3^2}$

$= 4$ ft

$CD = 4$ ft [given]

9. a) 1st pair: $\triangle ABC \cong \triangle ADC$

2nd pair: $\triangle ADE \cong \triangle CDE$

b) In $\triangle ABC$ and $\triangle ADC$,

$AB = AD$ [sides of rhombus]

$BC = DC$ [sides of rhombus]

$AC = AC$ [common side]

By the SSS test, $\triangle ABC \cong \triangle ADC$.

In $\triangle ADE$ and $\triangle CDE$,

$AD = CD$ [sides of rhombus]

$m\angle ADE = m\angle CDE$ [given]

$DE = DE$ [common side]

By the SAS test, $\triangle ADE \cong \triangle CDE$.

Lesson 9.2

1.

In $\triangle B$,

$u° = v°$

$= \dfrac{180° - 60°}{2}$ [base ∠s of isosceles △]

$= 60°$

In $\triangle D$,

$w° = x° = y° = 60°$ [∠s of an equilateral △]

At least two pairs of corresponding angles have equal measures. So, B ~ D.

2.

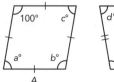

In A,

$c° = 180° - 100°$ [property of rhombus]

$= 80°$

$a° = c°$

$= 80°$ [property of rhombus]

$b° = 100°$ [property of rhombus]

In E,

$d° = 80°$ [opp. ∠s of ll gram)

$f° = 180° - 80°$ [int. ∠s of ll gram]

$= 100°$

$e° = f°$ [opp. ∠s of ll gram]

$= 100°$

So, $a° = c° = d° = 80°$

$b° = e° = f° = 100°$

All corresponding angles in A and E have equal measures. So, A ~ E.

3. Scale factor: $\dfrac{YX}{AB} = \dfrac{9}{6}$

$= 1.5$

4. Scale factor: $\dfrac{XZ}{AC} = \dfrac{17.5}{14}$

$= 1.25$

5. $m\angle X = m\angle A$

$x = 90$

$m\angle Y = 180° - m\angle X - m\angle Z$ [∠ sum of △]

$= 180° - 90° - 30°$

$= 60°$

$m\angle B = m\angle Y$

$b = 60$

So, $x = 90$ and $b = 60$.

6. $\dfrac{BC}{YZ} = \dfrac{AB}{XY}$

$\dfrac{a}{12} = \dfrac{10}{8}$

$12 \cdot \dfrac{a}{12} = \dfrac{10}{8} \cdot 12$

$a = 15$

$\dfrac{XZ}{AC} = \dfrac{XY}{AB}$

$\dfrac{y}{12} = \dfrac{8}{10}$

$12 \cdot \dfrac{y}{12} = \dfrac{8}{10} \cdot 12$

$y = 9.6$

So, $a = 15$ and $y = 9.6$.

7. $m\angle Y = m\angle B$

$\quad y = 120$

$\quad \dfrac{AB}{XY} = \dfrac{BC}{YZ}$

$\quad \dfrac{c}{39} = \dfrac{20}{30}$

$\quad 39 \cdot \dfrac{c}{39} = \dfrac{20}{30} \cdot 39$

$\quad\quad c = 26$

So, $y = 120$ and $c = 26$.

8. $m\angle D = m\angle S$

$\quad d = 130$

$\quad m\angle P = m\angle A = 90°$

$\quad m\angle Q = 360° - m\angle R - m\angle S - m\angle P$

$\quad\quad\quad\quad\quad$ [$\angle$ sum of quadrilateral]

$\quad q° = 360° - 60° - 130° - 90°$

$\quad q = 80$

$\quad \dfrac{PQ}{AB} = \dfrac{PS}{AD}$

$\quad \dfrac{x}{10} = \dfrac{12}{7.5}$

$\quad\quad x = \dfrac{12}{7.5} \cdot 10$

$\quad\quad\quad = 16$

So, $d = 130$, $q = 80$, and $x = 16$.

9. a) $\triangle ABD \sim \triangle DBC$

b) $\dfrac{AB}{DB} = \dfrac{4}{6} = \dfrac{2}{3}$

$\quad \dfrac{BD}{BC} = \dfrac{6}{9} = \dfrac{2}{3}$

$\quad \dfrac{AD}{DC} = \dfrac{5}{7.5} = \dfrac{2}{3}$

All three pairs of corresponding side lengths have the same ratio.
So, $\triangle ABD \sim \triangle DBC$.

10. a) $\triangle BAC \sim \triangle DEC$

b) $m\angle BAC = m\angle DEC$ [given]

$\quad m\angle ACB = m\angle ECD$ [vertically

$\quad\quad\quad\quad\quad\quad\quad$ opposite $\angle$s]

Two pairs of corresponding angles have equal measures.
So, $\triangle BAC \sim \triangle DEC$.

c) $\dfrac{CD}{CB} = \dfrac{DE}{BA}$

$\quad \dfrac{x}{1} = \dfrac{4.5}{1.5}$

$\quad\quad x = 3$

$\quad \dfrac{AC}{EC} = \dfrac{AB}{ED}$

$\quad \dfrac{y}{3.9} = \dfrac{1.5}{4.5}$

$\quad\quad y = \dfrac{1.5}{4.5} \cdot 3.9$

$\quad\quad\quad = 1.3$

So, $x = 3$ and $y = 1.3$.

11. a) $\triangle ABE \sim \triangle ACD$

b) $m\angle BAE = m\angle CAD$ [common $\angle$]

$\quad m\angle ABE = m\angle ACD$ [corresponding $\angle$s,

$\quad\quad\quad\quad\quad\quad\quad\quad$ BE ∥ CD]

Two pairs of corresponding angles have equal measures. So, $\triangle ABE \sim \triangle ACD$.

c) $\dfrac{BE}{CD} = \dfrac{AB}{AC}$

$\quad \dfrac{x}{10} = \dfrac{2}{5}$

$\quad 10 \cdot \dfrac{x}{10} = \dfrac{2}{5} \cdot 10$

$\quad\quad x = 4$

$\quad \dfrac{AD}{AE} = \dfrac{AC}{AB}$

$\quad \dfrac{y+3}{3} = \dfrac{5}{2}$

$\quad 3 \cdot \dfrac{y+3}{3} = \dfrac{5}{2} \cdot 3$

$\quad\quad y + 3 = 7.5$

$\quad y + 3 - 3 = 7.5 - 3$

$\quad\quad\quad y = 4.5$

So, $x = 4$ and $y = 4.5$.

12. a) $\triangle ABC \sim \triangle DEC$

b) $m\angle ACB = m\angle DCE$ [vertically

$\quad\quad\quad\quad\quad\quad\quad$ opposite $\angle$s]

$\quad m\angle BAC = m\angle EDC$ [alternate $\angle$s,

$\quad\quad\quad\quad\quad\quad\quad$ BA ∥ DE]

Two pairs of corresponding angles have equal measures. So, $\triangle ABC \sim \triangle DEC$.

c) $\dfrac{CD}{CA} = \dfrac{DE}{AB}$

$\quad \dfrac{CD}{7.2} = \dfrac{2}{8}$

$\quad 7.2 \cdot \dfrac{CD}{7.2} = \dfrac{2}{8} \cdot 7.2$

$\quad\quad CD = 1.8$

$\quad\quad AD = 7.2 + 1.8$

$\quad\quad\quad = 9$ in.

So, length of $\overline{AD} = 9$ in.

$\quad \dfrac{BC}{EC} = \dfrac{AB}{DE}$

$\quad \dfrac{BC}{1.5} = \dfrac{8}{2}$

$\quad 1.5 \cdot \dfrac{BC}{1.5} = \dfrac{8}{2} \cdot 1.5$

$\quad\quad BC = 6$ in.

$\quad BE = 6 + 1.5$

$\quad\quad = 7.5$ in.

So, length of $\overline{BE} = 7.5$ in.

13. For Figure B:

  a) Figure B is a reduction of Figure A.

  b) Scale factor $= \dfrac{8}{10}$

    $= 0.8$

  c) Since Figure A and Figure B are similar,

    $\dfrac{x}{5} = \dfrac{8}{10}$

    $5 \cdot \dfrac{x}{5} = \dfrac{8}{10} \cdot 5$

    $x = 4$

For Figure C:

  a) Figure C is an enlargement of Figure A.

  b) Scale factor $= \dfrac{7.5}{5}$

    $= 1.5$

  c) Since Figure B and Figure C are similar,

    $\dfrac{y}{4} = 1.5$

    $4 \cdot \dfrac{y}{4} = 1.5 \cdot 4$

    $y = 6$

14. a) Scale factor $= \dfrac{XY}{AB}$

    $= \dfrac{18}{12}$

    $= \dfrac{3}{2}$ or 1.5

  b) $\dfrac{YZ}{BC} = 1.5$

    $\dfrac{YZ}{8} = 1.5$

    $8 \cdot \dfrac{YZ}{8} = 1.5 \cdot 8$

    $YZ = 12$

    So, the length of $\overline{YZ}$ is 12 inches.

  c) $\dfrac{\text{Area of } \triangle XYZ}{\text{Area of } \triangle ABC} = (\text{scale factor})^2$

    $\dfrac{\text{Area of } \triangle XYZ}{48} = \left(\dfrac{3}{2}\right)^2$

    Area of $\triangle XYZ = \dfrac{9}{4} \cdot 48$

    $= 108 \text{ in}^2$

    The area of $\triangle XYZ$ is 108 square inches.

15. a) $m\angle XOY = m\angle POQ$ [common $\angle$]

    $m\angle OPQ = m\angle OXY$ [corresponding
    $\angle$s, $PQ \parallel XY$]

    $m\angle OQP = m\angle OYX$ [corresponding
    $\angle$s, $PQ \parallel XY$]

    All corresponding angles have equal
    measures. So, $\triangle OPQ \sim \triangle OXY$.

    $\dfrac{XY}{PQ} = \dfrac{OX}{OP}$

    $\dfrac{XY}{16} = \dfrac{15}{9}$

    $16 \cdot \dfrac{XY}{16} = \dfrac{15}{9} \cdot 16$

    $XY = 26\dfrac{2}{3}$

    So, the length of $\overline{XY}$ is $26\dfrac{2}{3}$ feet.

  b) Let the area of $\triangle OPQ$ be A ft².

    $\dfrac{\text{Area of } \triangle OXY}{\text{Area of } \triangle OPQ} = \left(\dfrac{OX}{OP}\right)^2$

    $\dfrac{\text{Area of } \triangle OXY}{A} = \left(\dfrac{15}{9}\right)^2$

    Area of $\triangle OXY = \left(\dfrac{15}{9}\right)^2 A$

    $= \left(\dfrac{5}{3}\right)^2 A \text{ ft}^2$

    Area of trapezoid $PQYX = \left(\dfrac{5}{3}\right)^2 A - A$

    $= \dfrac{25}{9} A$

    Area of $\triangle OPQ$: Area of trapezoid $PQYX$

    $A : \dfrac{25}{9} A$

    $9A : 25A$

    $9 : 25$

  c) $\dfrac{\text{Area of trapezoid } PQYX}{\text{Area of } \triangle OPQ} = \dfrac{25}{9}$

    $\dfrac{\text{Area of trapezoid } PQYX}{80} = \dfrac{25}{9}$

    Area of trapezoid $PQYX = \dfrac{25}{9} \cdot 80$

    $= 222\dfrac{2}{9} \text{ ft}^2$

    The area of trapezoid $PQYX$

    is $222\dfrac{2}{9}$ square feet.

16. Let the height of the lamp-post be h feet.

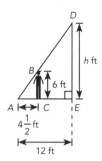

m∠DAE = m∠BAC [common ∠]
m∠ADE = m∠ABC [corresponding ∠s,
            BC ∥ DE]
Two pairs of corresponding angles have
equal measures. So, △ABC ∼ △ADE.

$$\frac{DE}{BC} = \frac{AE}{AC}$$

$$\frac{h}{6} = \frac{12}{4\frac{1}{2}}$$

$$6 \cdot \frac{h}{6} = \frac{12}{\frac{9}{2}} \cdot 6$$

$$h = \frac{8}{3} \cdot 6$$

$$h = 16$$

The height of the lamp-post is 16 feet.

17. a) Since △PQR ∼ △ABC,

$$\frac{PQ}{AB} = \frac{QR}{BC}$$

$$\frac{PQ}{7.5} = \frac{6}{10}$$

$$7.5 \cdot \frac{PQ}{7.5} = \frac{6}{10} \cdot 7.5$$

$$PQ = 4.5$$

In △PQR, $PR^2 = PQ^2 + QR^2$
$$PR^2 = 4.5^2 + 6^2$$
$$PR = \sqrt{4.5^2 + 6^2}$$
$$= 7.5 \text{ cm}$$

Perimeter of inner triangle
= 6 + 4.5 + 7.5
= 18 cm
The perimeter of the inner triangle is
18 centimeters.

b) Area of △ABC = $\frac{1}{2} \cdot 10 \cdot 7.5$
$$= 37.5 \text{ cm}^2$$

Area of △PQR = $\frac{1}{2} \cdot 6 \cdot 4.5$
$$= 13.5 \text{ cm}^2$$

Area of remaining block = 37.5 – 13.5
$$= 24 \text{ cm}^2$$
The area of the remaining block is
24 square centimeters.

18. m∠PXA = m∠BXQ [vertically opposite ∠s]
m∠APB = m∠QBX [alternate ∠s, PA ∥ BQ]
Two pairs of corresponding angles have
equal measures. So, △AXP ∼ △QXB.

$$\frac{PX}{BX} = \frac{PA}{BQ}$$

$$\frac{PX}{10} = \frac{24}{12}$$

$$10 \cdot \frac{PX}{10} = \frac{24}{12} \cdot 10$$

$$PX = 20 \text{ ft}$$

Length of the pole $\overline{BP}$ = 10 + 20
$$= 30 \text{ ft}$$
The length of pole $\overline{BP}$ is 30 feet.
In △PAB, $AB^2 = PB^2 - PA^2$
$$AB^2 = 30^2 - 24^2$$
$$AB = \sqrt{30^2 - 24^2}$$
$$= 18 \text{ ft}$$
The distance between the walls is 18 feet.
In △ABQ, $AQ^2 = AB^2 + BQ^2$
$$AQ^2 = 18^2 + 12^2$$
$$AQ = \sqrt{18^2 + 12^2}$$
$$= 21.63$$
$$≈ 21.6 \text{ ft}$$
The length of pole $\overline{AQ}$ is 21.6 feet.

19. a) m∠AOB = m∠DOC [vertically
                    opposite ∠s]
m∠ABO = m∠DCO [alternate ∠s,
                    AB ∥ CD]
Two pairs of corresponding angles have
equal measures. So, △AOB ∼ △DOC.
m∠COD = m∠EOF [common ∠]
m∠OCD = m∠OEF [corresponding ∠s,
                    CD ∥ EF]
Two pairs of corresponding angles have
equal measures. So, △OCD ∼ △OEF.
m∠AOB = m∠FOE [vertically
                    opposite ∠s]
m∠ABO = m∠FEO [alternate ∠s,
                    AB ∥ EF]
Two pairs of corresponding angles have
equal measures. So, △AOB ∼ △FEO.
                    [equiangular]

b) △AOE is not similar to △BOF.
Only one pair of angles (∠AOE and
∠BOF) are equal. The remaining two
pairs are not equal.
△AOE is not similar to △BOF.

Lesson 9.3

1. Congruent
2. Congruent
3. Similar
4. Congruent
5. Similar
6. a) △ABC is mapped onto △A′B′C′ by using a reflection in the line y = x. △A′B′C′ is mapped onto △A″B″C″ by using a rotation of 90° clockwise about the point (0, 0).

b)

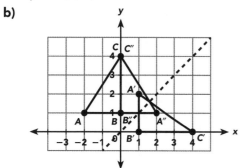

c) No; the coordinates are different because the order of transformations is reversed. Yes; the size and shape of figures remain the same under translations and reflections.

7. a)

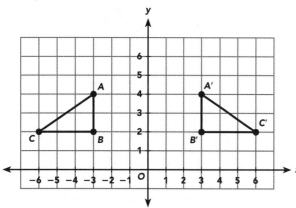

b) △A′B′C is mapped onto △A″B″C″ by a rotation of 90° clockwise about origin O.

c) A reflection about the line y = x will map △ABC onto △A″B″C″.

8. a)

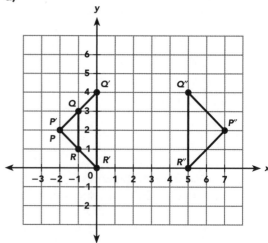

b) △P′Q′R is mapped onto △P″Q″R″ by a reflection about the line x = 2.5.

c) A dilation of scale factor −2 about the point (1, 2) will map △PQR to △P″Q″R″.

9. a) △ABC is mapped onto △A′B′C′ by a translation of 4 units to the right and 6 units up.
△A′B′C′ is mapped onto △A″B″C″ by a rotation of 90° clockwise about the point (0, 2).

b) △ABC is mapped onto △A′B′C′ by a reflection about the line x = −1. △A′B′C′ is mapped onto △A″B″C″ by a dilation of scale factor −3 about the point (−1, 1).

c) △ABC is mapped onto △A′B′C′ by a rotation of 90° counter clockwise about the point (−2, 0). △A′B′C′ is mapped onto △A″B″C″ by a reflection about the line y = x.

10. a) m∠QRS = m∠BCD
$$= 360° - m∠DAB - m∠ABC - m∠CDA \quad [∠\text{sum of quadrilateral}]$$
$$= 360° - 90° - 120° - 80°$$
$$= 70°$$

b) $\dfrac{PQ}{AB} = 1.5$ (scale factor)

$\dfrac{PQ}{3} = 1.5$

$3 \cdot \dfrac{PQ}{3} = 3 \cdot 1.5$

$PQ = 4.5$

The length of $\overline{PQ}$ is 4.5 feet.

c) $\dfrac{\text{Area of } PQRS}{\text{Area of } ABCD} = (1.5)^2$

$\dfrac{\text{Area of } PQRS}{12} = (1.5)^2$

$\text{Area of } PQRS = (1.5)^2 \cdot 12$

$= 27 \text{ ft}^2$

The area of $PQRS$ is 27 square feet.

11. Let the scale factor be k.

$\dfrac{\text{Area of enlarged copy}}{\text{Area of original postcard}} = k^2$

$\dfrac{240}{60} = k^2$

$4 = k^2$

$k = 2$

The diagonal of the postcard is dilated by a scale factor of 2.

Brain @ Work

1. Let the height of the big triangle be p.

$\dfrac{p}{4+m} = \dfrac{3}{4}$

$4p = 3(4 + m)$

$4p = 12 + 3m$ — Eq. 1

$\dfrac{p}{n+4+m} = \dfrac{3}{5}$

$5p = 3(n + 4 + m)$

$5p = 3n + 12 + 3m$

$5p = 3m + 3n + 12$ — Eq. 2

Multiply Eq. 1 by 5:

$5 \cdot 4p = 5 \cdot (12 + 3m)$

$20p = 60 + 15m$ — Eq. 3

Multiply Eq. 2 by 4:

$4 \cdot 5p = 4 \cdot (3m + 3n + 12)$

$20p = 12m + 12n + 48$ — Eq. 4

Substitute Eq. 3 into Eq. 4:

$60 + 15m = 12m + 12n + 48$

$60 + 15m - 60 = 12m + 12n + 48 - 60$

$15m = 12m + 12n - 12$

$15m - 12m = 12m + 12n - 12 - 12m$

$3m = 12n - 12$

$\dfrac{3m}{3} = \dfrac{12n - 12}{3}$

$m = 4n - 4$

2. $\angle XAY = \angle BAZ$ [common angle]

$\angle AYX = \angle AZB$ [corr. $\angle$s]

$\triangle XAY$ and $\triangle BAZ$ are similar.

$\dfrac{AY}{AZ} = \dfrac{XY}{BZ}$

$\dfrac{AZ}{BZ} = \dfrac{AY}{XY}$

$\angle XBW = \angle ABZ$ [common angle]

$\angle BWX = \angle BZA$ [corr. $\angle$s]

$\triangle XBW$ and $\triangle ABZ$ are similar.

$\dfrac{BW}{BZ} = \dfrac{XW}{AZ}$

$\dfrac{AZ}{BZ} = \dfrac{XW}{BW}$

So, $\dfrac{AY}{XY} = \dfrac{XW}{BW}$.

Since $XW = YZ$ and $WZ = XY$,

$\dfrac{AY}{WZ} = \dfrac{YZ}{BW}$

$\dfrac{AY}{YZ} = \dfrac{ZW}{WV}$

So, $AY : YZ = ZW : WB$. (shown)

Cumulative Practice for Chapters 7 to 9

1. $p^2 = 26^2 + 24^2$

$p^2 = 676 + 576$

$p^2 = 1{,}252$

$p = \sqrt{1{,}252}$

$p \approx 35.4$

2. $13^2 = 5^2 + x^2$

$169 = 25 + x^2$

$169 - 25 = 25 + x^2 - 25$

$144 = x^2$

$x = \sqrt{144}$

$x = 12$

$y^2 = x^2 + 16^2$

$y^2 = 12^2 + 16^2$

$y^2 = 144 + 256$

$y^2 = 400$

$y = \sqrt{400}$

$y = 20$

3. $26^2 \overset{?}{=} 24^2 + 7^2$

$676 \overset{?}{=} 576 + 49$

$676 \neq 625$

The triangle is not a right triangle.

4. $12.5^2 \overset{?}{=} 10^2 + 7.5^2$

$156.25 \overset{?}{=} 100 + 56.25$

$156.25 = 156.25$

The triangle is a right triangle.

5. Distance from E to F
$$= \sqrt{(x_2 - x_1)^2 + (y_2 - y_1)^2}$$
$$= \sqrt{(5 - 3)^2 + (11 - 2)^2}$$
$$= \sqrt{2^2 + 9^2}$$
$$= \sqrt{4 + 81}$$
$$= \sqrt{85}$$
$$\approx 9.2 \text{ units}$$

6. Distance from M to N
$$= \sqrt{(x_2 - x_1)^2 + (y_2 - y_1)^2}$$
$$= \sqrt{[4 - (-2)]^2 + (0 - 6)^2}$$
$$= \sqrt{6^2 + (-6)^2}$$
$$= \sqrt{36 + 36}$$
$$= \sqrt{72}$$
$$\approx 8.5 \text{ units}$$

7. $8^2 = x^2 + x^2$
$2x^2 = 64$
$\dfrac{2x^2}{2} = \dfrac{64}{2}$
$x^2 = 32$
$x = \sqrt{32}$
$x \approx 5.7$

8. $a^2 = 12^2 + 5^2$
$a^2 = 144 + 25$
$a^2 = 169$
$a = \sqrt{169}$
$a = 13$

9. Let the radius of the cone be x inches.
$$25^2 = 20^2 + x^2$$
$$625 = 400 + x^2$$
$$625 - 400 = 400 + x^2 - 400$$
$$225 = x^2$$
$$x = \sqrt{225}$$
$$x = 15$$
Volume of cone $= \dfrac{1}{3}\pi r^2 h$
$$\approx \dfrac{1}{3} \cdot 3.14 \cdot 15^2 \cdot 20$$
$$= 4{,}710 \text{ in}^3$$
Volume of hemisphere $= \dfrac{1}{2} \cdot \left(\dfrac{4}{3}\pi r^3\right)$
$$\approx \dfrac{1}{2} \cdot \left(\dfrac{4}{3} \cdot 3.14 \cdot 15^3\right)$$
$$= 7{,}065 \text{ in}^3$$
Volume of composite solid
$= 4{,}710 + 7{,}065$
$= 11{,}775 \text{ in}^3$
The volume of the composite solid is 11,775 cubic inches.

10. Let half of the side length of the cube be x inches.
$$22.5^2 = 19^2 + x^2$$
$$506.25 = 361 + x^2$$
$$506.25 - 361 = 361 + x^2 - 361$$
$$145.25 = x^2$$
$$x = \sqrt{145.25}$$
$$x \approx 12.05$$
Side length of cube $= 2 \cdot 12.05$
$$= 24.1 \text{ in.}$$
Volume of cube $= (24.1)^3$
$$\approx 13{,}997.52 \text{ in}^3$$
Volume of square pyramid $= \dfrac{1}{3} \cdot (2x)^2 \cdot h$
$$= \dfrac{1}{3} \cdot (24.1)^2 \cdot 19$$
$$\approx 3{,}678.46 \text{ in}^3$$
Volume of composite solid
$= 13{,}997.52 + 3{,}678.46$
$\approx 17{,}676.0 \text{ in}^3$
The volume of the composite solid is approximately 17,676.0 cubic inches.

11. $(5 + 3, -3 - 2) = (8, -5)$
$X (5, -3)$ is mapped onto $(8, -5)$.

12. $(-8 - 6, 7 + 4) = (-14, 11)$
$Y (-8, 7)$ is mapped onto $(-14, 11)$.

13.

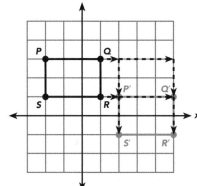

14.

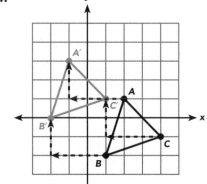

15.

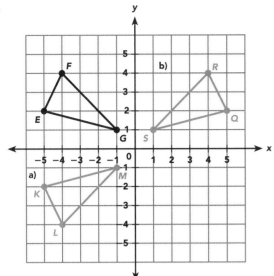

16. a) 90° clockwise about (0, 0) or
270° counterclockwise about (0, 0)
b) 180° about (0, 0)

17.

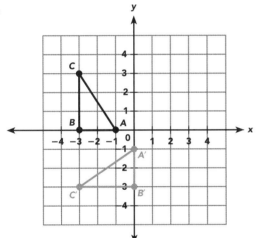

18. *ABCD* is not a dilation of *EBFD*. The lengths
of the corresponding sides are not in the
same ratio.

19. △*X′Y′Z′* is a dilation of △*XYZ* with center
(2, 3) and a scale factor of $\frac{1}{2}$.

20. a)

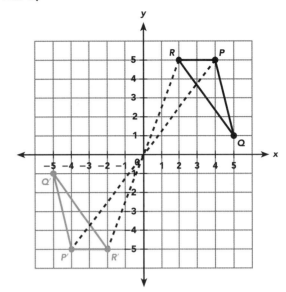

b)

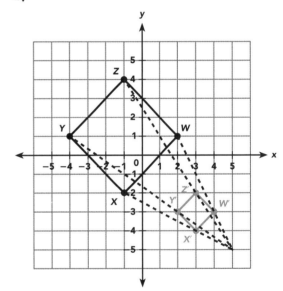

21. a) 90° counterclockwise about (0, 0) or
270° clockwise about (0, 0)
b) Triangle R is a dilation of triangle Q with
center (−6, −5) and a scale factor of 4.

22. m∠*RPQ* = m∠*UVT* = 55°
SU = *PR*
ST = *PQ*
By the SAS test, △*PQR* ≅ △*STU*.

23. $DF = AC$
$x + 4 = 11$
$x = 7$
$\angle E = \angle B$
$8x + 3y = 92$
$8(7) + 3y = 92$
$56 + 3y - 56 = 92 - 56$
$3y = 36$
$y = 12$
So, $x = 7$, $y = 12$.

24. $\dfrac{JL}{JK} = \dfrac{GI}{GH}$

$\dfrac{p}{5} = \dfrac{9.6}{12}$

$5 \cdot \dfrac{p}{5} = \dfrac{9.6}{12} \cdot 5$

$p = 4$

25. We can use the AAA test to determine whether the two triangles are similar.

$\dfrac{x}{24} = \dfrac{8.4}{28}$

$24 \cdot \dfrac{x}{24} = \dfrac{8.4}{28} \cdot 24$

$x = 7.2$

26.

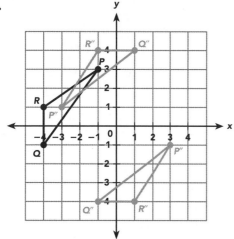

a) P'' (3, −1), Q'' (−1, −4), R'' (1, −4)
b) P'' (−3, 1), Q'' (1, 4), R'' (−1, 4)
c) Yes. Reflections and rotations result in congruent figures.
d) Reflection in the line $y = x$
e) Reflection in the line $y = -x$

27. Let x be the diameter of the glass.
$19.5^2 = x^2 + 18^2$
$380.25 = x^2 + 324$
$380.25 - 324 = x^2 + 324 - 324$
$56.25 = x^2$
$x = \sqrt{56.25}$
$x = 7.5$
Radius $= \dfrac{7.5}{2}$
$= 3.75$
The radius of the glass is 3.75 centimeters.

28. Let the diagonal length of the television be y inches.
$y^2 = 33.6^2 + 25.2^2$
$y^2 = 1{,}128.96 + 635.04$
$y^2 = 1{,}764$
$y = \sqrt{1{,}764}$
$y = 42$
The size of the television set is 42 inches.

29. a) The shape $HEFG$ is congruent to $ABCD$.
b) $BC = EF$
$4n = 8$
$\dfrac{4n}{4} = \dfrac{8}{4}$
$n = 2$
$CD = FG$
$7 = 5p + 3$
$7 - 3 = 5p + 3 - 3$
$4 = 5p$
$\dfrac{4}{5} = \dfrac{5p}{5}$
$p = \dfrac{4}{5}$

$DA = GH$

$2 + \dfrac{3}{2}m = 2m - 1$

$2 + \dfrac{3}{2}m + 1 = 2m - 1 + 1$

$3 + \dfrac{3}{2}m = 2m$

$3 + \dfrac{3}{2}m - \dfrac{3}{2}m = 2m - \dfrac{3}{2}m$

$3 = 2m - \dfrac{3}{2}m$

$3 = \dfrac{m}{2}$

$2 \cdot 3 = \dfrac{m}{2} \cdot 2$

$m = 6$

30. a) Volume of cone $= \frac{1}{3}\pi r^2 h$

$$16 \approx \frac{1}{3}(3.14)r^2(6.2)$$

$$16 = \frac{19.468}{3}r^2$$

$$3 \cdot 16 = \frac{19.468}{3}r^2 \cdot 3$$

$$48 = 19.468r^2$$

$$\frac{48}{19.468} = \frac{19.468r^2}{19.468}$$

$$r^2 = \frac{48}{19.468}$$

$$r \approx 1.57$$

The radius of the cone is 1.57 centimeters.

b) Let the slant height of the cone be
l centimeters.
$l^2 = 1.57^2 + 6.2^2$
$l^2 = 40.9049$
$l = \sqrt{40.9049}$
$l \approx 6.396$ in.
Curved surface area of cone
$= \pi r l$
$\approx 3.14 \cdot 1.57 \cdot 6.396$
≈ 31.53 in²
Curved surface of cylinder
$= 2\pi r h$
$\approx 2 \cdot 3.14 \cdot 1.57 \cdot 6.2$
≈ 61.13 in²
Base area of cylinder
$= \pi r^2$
$\approx 3.14 \cdot 1.57^2$
≈ 7.74 in²
Total surface area of remaining solid
$= 31.53 + 61.13 + 7.74$
$= 100.4$
≈ 100 in²
The total surface area of the remaining
solid is approximately 100 square inches.

31. a) Base area of bigger pyramid = 144 cm²
So, the side length of the base of the
bigger pyramid = $\sqrt{144}$ = 12 cm
Let the slant height of the bigger
pyramid be x.
Then the slant height of the smaller
pyramid is $\frac{x}{2}$.

By Pythagorean Theorem, $x^2 = 8^2 + \left(\frac{12}{2}\right)^2$

$$x^2 = 64 + 36$$
$$x^2 = 100$$
$$x = \sqrt{100}$$
$$x = 10$$

Slant height $= \frac{x}{2}$

$$= \frac{10}{2}$$

$$= 5 \text{ cm}$$

So, the slant height of the smaller
pyramid is 5 centimeters.

b) Surface area of bigger pyramid
= Base area + Area of 4 triangular faces

$$= 144 + 4\left(\frac{1}{2} \cdot 12 \cdot 10\right)$$

$$= 144 + 4(60)$$
$$= 144 + 240$$
$$= 384 \text{ cm}^2$$
Surface area of smaller pyramid
= Base area + Area of 4 triangular faces

$$= (6 \cdot 6) + 4\left(\frac{1}{2} \cdot 6 \cdot 5\right)$$

$$= 36 + 4(15)$$
$$= 36 + 60$$
$$= 96 \text{ cm}^2$$
Surface area of . Surface area of
bigger pyramid ˙ smaller pyramid
384 : 96
4 : 1
The ratio of surface areas of the bigger
pyramid to the smaller pyramid is 4 to 1.

32. 10 cm → 78 ft

$$4.6 \text{ cm} \rightarrow \frac{78}{10} \cdot 4.6$$

$$= 35.88 \text{ ft}$$

The actual width of the tennis court
is 35.88 feet.

33. a) Since $DE = KH$, $EF = HI$, $FG = IJ$,
$GD = JK$, $DEFG$ and $KHIJ$ are congruent.
b) m∠$JST = 180° - 45°$
$= 135°$
c) $STUV$ is rotated 180° about the center
S to $KHIJ$.

Chapter 10

Lesson 10.1

1.

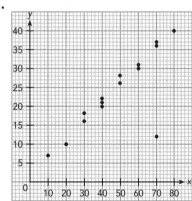

2.

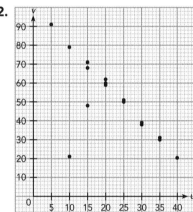

3.

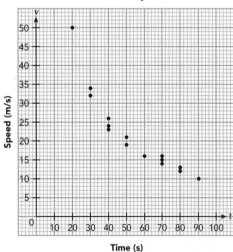

Time and Speed

4. No association

5. Strong, negative, and linear association

6. Strong, positive, and nonlinear association

7. Strong, positive, and nonlinear association

8. (1, 2)

9. (1, 7) and (5, 1)

10.

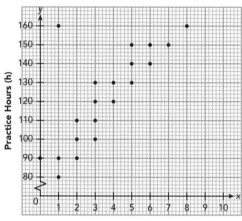

11. (1, 160). The outlier could represent a season where the players in the team were mainly rookies, or did not work well together despite practising very hard.

12. With the exception of the outlier, there is a strong, positive, and linear association.

13.

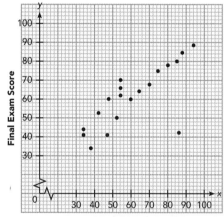

Mathematics Examination

14. (86, 41). The outlier could represent a student who is fairly competent in Mathematics (Midterm: 86 marks), but who performed poorly on the Final Exam (41 marks) due to missing too many classes before the Final Exam.

15. With the exception of the outlier, there is a strong, positive, and linear association between the Midterm scores and the Final Exam scores, as the points cluster along a straight line with a positive slope.

Lesson 10.2

1. Line B

2. Line R

3.

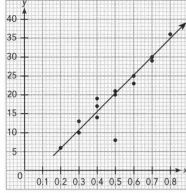

4.

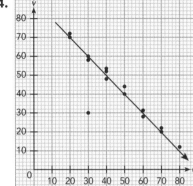

5. **Time and Distance**

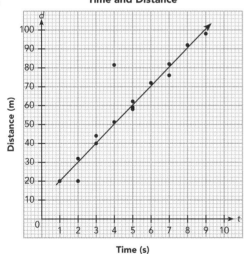

6. **Productivity**

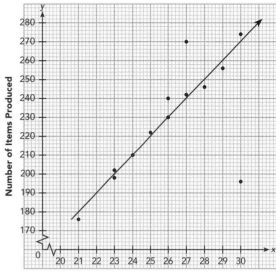

Using the points (24, 210) and (26, 230):

$$m = \frac{230 - 210}{26 - 24} = \frac{20}{2} = 10$$

Using the equation in slope-intercept form:

$$y = mx + b$$
$$230 = 10(26) + b$$
$$230 = 260 + b$$
$$230 - 260 = 260 + b - 260$$
$$b = -30$$

Equation of line of best fit:

$$y = mx + b$$
$$y = 10x - 30$$

The equation of the line of best fit is
$y = 10x - 30$.

7. **Cost of Manufacturing**

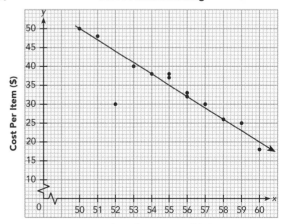

Using the points (50, 50) and (54, 38):

$$m = \frac{50 - 38}{50 - 54} = -3$$

Using the equation in slope-intercept form:

$$y = mx + b$$
$$38 = -3(54) + b$$
$$38 = -162 + b$$
$$38 + 162 = -162 + b + 162$$
$$200 = b$$

Equation of line of best fit:

$$y = -3x + 200$$

The equation of the line of best fit is $y = -3x + 200$.

8 & 9.

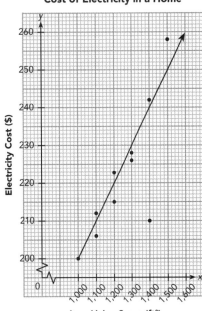

Cost of Electricity in a Home

10. Using the points (1,000, 200) and (1,500, 250):

$$m = \frac{250 - 200}{1,500 - 1,000} = 0.1$$

Using the equation in slope-intercept form:

$$y = mx + b$$
$$250 = 0.1(1,500) + b$$
$$250 = 150 + b$$
$$250 - 150 = 150 + b - 150$$
$$100 = b$$

Equation of line of best fit:

$$y = 0.1x + 100$$

The equation of the line of best fit is $y = 0.1x + 100$.

11. There is a strong, positive, and linear association between area of living space within a home and cost of electricity.

12. (1,400, 210): The family in this home could have gone on vacation for the month or they are using an alternative type of energy.

13. $235
14. 1,300 ft²

Lesson 10.3

1. Hobby
2. Color
3. Categorical
4. Quantitative
5. Quantitative
6. $x + 5 = 125$
    $x + 5 - 5 = 125 - 5$
        $x = 120$

120 student passed both Mathematics and Science.

7. $y + 5 = 15$
    $y + 5 - 5 = 15 - 5$
        $y = 10$

10 students failed both Mathematics and Science.

8. $125 + t = 160$
    $125 + t - 125 = 160 - 125$
            $t = 35$

35 students failed Science.

9.

Plays Basketball

	Yes	No	Total
Yes	3	15	18
No	10	2	12
Total	13	17	30

Plays Volleyball

10. The statement "Most of the members play one of the two games" is true. Out of the 30 members, 25 play only one of the 2 games; 15 play only basketball and 10 play only volleyball.

11. No. Generally members who play basketball do not play volleyball and vice versa, as only 3 out of the 30 members play both games.

12.

Plays International Chess

		Yes	No	Total
Plays Chinese Chess	**Yes**	$\frac{40}{42} \approx 0.95$	$\frac{2}{42} \approx 0.05$	1
	No	$\frac{3}{8} = 0.375$	$\frac{5}{8} \approx 0.625$	1

Among those who play Chinese, the majority (95%) also play International Chess. Among those who do not play Chinese Chess, most (62.5%) do not play International Chess either.

13.

Plays International Chess

		Yes	No
Plays Chinese Chess	**Yes**	$\frac{40}{43} \approx 0.93$	$\frac{2}{7} \approx 0.29$
	No	$\frac{3}{43} \approx 0.07$	$\frac{5}{7} \approx 0.71$
	Total	1	1

Among those who play International Chess, the majority (93%) also play Chinese Chess. Among those who do not play International Chess, most (71%) do not play Chinese Chess either.

14. Generally a member who plays Chinese Chess also plays International Chess (95%) and a member who plays International Chess also plays Chinese Chess (93%).

Brain @ Work

$y = x$ — Eq. 1

$z = 3x + 2$ — Eq. 2

Substitute Eq. 1 into Eq. 2:

$z = 3y + 2$

So, there is a linear association between y and z.

Chapter 11

Lesson 11.1

1. True
2. False
3. True
4. False

---

5. Simple event
6. Compound event
   The two simple events are:
   - drawing a black pebble from the bag of 10 pebbles and;
   - drawing a white pebble from the bag with the remaining 9 pebbles.
7. Simple event
8. Compound event
   The two simple events are:
   - rolling the 1st die and;
   - rolling the 2nd die.

9. a)

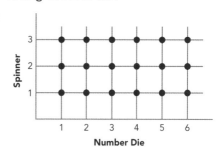

b) There are 18 outcomes.

10. a)

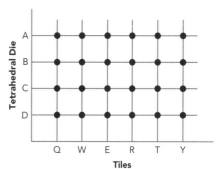

b) There are 24 outcomes.

11. a)

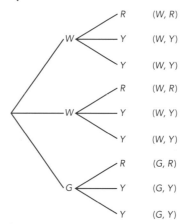

W represents white
R represents red
G represents green
Y represents yellow

b) There are 9 outcomes.

12. a)

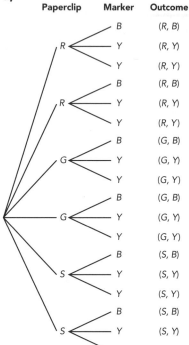

Paperclip	Marker	Outcome
R	B	(R, B)
	Y	(R, Y)
	Y	(R, Y)
R	B	(R, B)
	Y	(R, Y)
	Y	(R, Y)
G	B	(G, B)
	Y	(G, Y)
	Y	(G, Y)
G	B	(G, B)
	Y	(G, Y)
	Y	(G, Y)
S	B	(S, B)
	Y	(S, Y)
	Y	(S, Y)
S	B	(S, B)
	Y	(S, Y)
	Y	(S, Y)

R represents red
G represents green
S represents silver
B represents black
Y represents yellow

b) There are 18 outcomes.

13. a)

Six-Sided Number Die

+	**1**	**2**	**3**	**4**	**5**	**6**
1	②	3	④	5	⑥	7
2	3	④	5	⑥	7	⑧
3	④	5	⑥	7	⑧	9
4	5	⑥	7	⑧	9	⑩

Four-Sided Number Die (row labels)

The outcomes for an even sum is 12.

b) The outcomes with a sum greater than 6 is 10.

c) The outcomes for the sum being a prime number is 11, whereas the outcomes for a sum being a composite number is 13. So, there are more favorable outcomes for the sum being a composite number.

14. a)

Locker Combination

·	**1**	**2**	**3**	**4**	**5**	**6**
1	①	2	③	4	⑤	6
2	2	4	6	8	10	12
3	③	6	⑨	12	⑮	18
4	4	8	12	16	20	24
5	⑤	10	⑮	20	㉕	30
6	6	12	18	24	30	36

Computer Password (row labels)

b) The outcomes with a product greater than 20 is 6.

c) The outcomes with an odd product is 9.

Lesson 11.2

1. a)

Bag A

	B	**G**	**G**	**G**
G	(B, G)	G, G	G, G	G, G
B	B, B	(G, B)	(G, B)	(G, B)
B	B, B	(G, B)	(G, B)	(G, B)
B	B, B	(G, B)	(G, B)	(G, B)

Bag B (row labels)

Key: B represents blue
G represents green

b) There is a total of 16 outcomes.
The number of favorable outcomes is 10.
P(marbles are of different colors)
$$= \frac{10}{16}$$
$$= \frac{5}{8}$$

2.

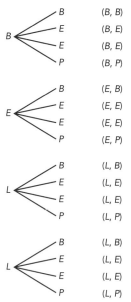

1st Word	2nd Word	Outcome
B	B	(B, B)
	E	(B, E)
	E	(B, E)
	P	(B, P)
E	B	(E, B)
	E	(E, E)
	E	(E, E)
	P	(E, P)
L	B	(L, B)
	E	(L, E)
	E	(L, E)
	P	(L, P)
L	B	(L, B)
	E	(L, E)
	E	(L, E)
	P	(L, P)

The outcomes for both letters chosen to be the same is 3.

3.

Die

Pens	1	2	3	4	5	6
B	B1	B2	B3	B4	B5	B6
G	G1	(G2)	G3	(G4)	G5	(G6)
G	G1	(G2)	G3	(G4)	G5	(G6)

Key: B represents blue
G represents green

There are 18 outcomes.
The number of favorable outcomes, green and even, is 6.

P(green and even) = $\frac{6}{18}$

= $\frac{1}{3}$

4.

Red Die

Yellow Die	+	1	2	3	4
	1	2	3	4	5
	2	3	4	5	(6)
	3	4	5	(6)	(7)
	4	5	(6)	(7)	(8)

There are 16 outcomes.
The number of favorable outcomes, sum is at least 6, is 6.

P(sum at least 6) = $\frac{6}{16}$

= $\frac{3}{8}$

5.

Type of Juice

Tin Size	A	A	A	G	G	O
S	(SA)	(SA)	(SA)	SG	SG	SO
M	MA	MA	MA	MG	MG	MO
L	LA	LA	LA	LG	LG	LO

Key: A represents apple
G represents grape
O represents orange
S represents small
M represents medium
L represents large

Total number of possible outcomes = 18
The number of favorable outcomes, small bottle of apple juice, is 3.

P(small bottle of apple juice) = $\frac{3}{18}$

= $\frac{1}{6}$

6. a)

Cards

Beads	·	1	2	4	6
	1	1	2	4	(6)
	3	3	(6)	12	18
	5	(5)	(10)	15	20

b) Total number of possible outcomes = 12
The number of favorable outcomes, product greater than or equal to 5 and less than or equal to 10, is 4.
P(product greater than or equal to 5 and less than or equal to 10)

= $\frac{4}{12}$

= $\frac{1}{3}$

7.

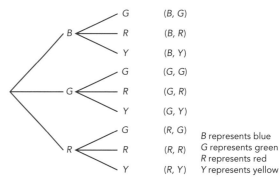

Bucket A Bucket B Outcome

B → G (B, G)
B → R (B, R)
B → Y (B, Y)
G → G (G, G)
G → R (G, R)
G → Y (G, Y)
R → G (R, G)
R → R (R, R)
R → Y (R, Y)

B represents blue
G represents green
R represents red
Y represents yellow

Total number of possible outcomes = 9
The number of favorable outcomes, both of the same color, is 2.

P(both of the same color) = $\frac{2}{9}$

8.

Die

Disc		1	1	3	4
	B	(B1)	(B1)	B3	B4
	B	(B1)	(B1)	B3	B4
	R	R1	R1	R3	R4

Key: B represents blue
R represents red

Total number of possible outcomes = 12
The number of favorable outcomes, drawing a blue disc and getting a 1, is 4.

P(a blue disc and 1) = $\frac{4}{12}$

= $\frac{1}{3}$

9.

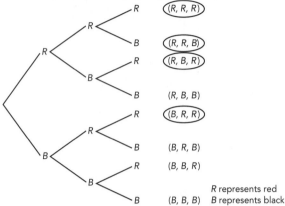

Total number of possible outcomes = 8
The number of favorable outcomes, more red tissue than black, is 4.

$$P(\text{more red tissue than black}) = \frac{4}{8}$$
$$= \frac{1}{2}$$

10. Let the letters be A, B, and C.

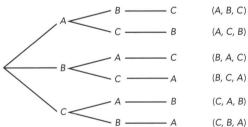

Envelope 1	Envelope 2	Envelope 3	Outcome
A	B ——— C		(A, B, C)
	C ——— B		(A, C, B)
B	A ——— C		(B, A, C)
	C ——— A		(B, C, A)
C	A ——— B		(C, A, B)
	B ——— A		(C, B, A)

P(correct letters in the correct envelopes) = $\frac{1}{6}$

Lesson 11.3

1.

Balloon	Number Die	Outcome
B	1	(B, 1)
	2	(B, 2)
	3	(B, 3)
	4	(B, 4)
	5	(B, 5)
	6	(B, 6)
W	1	(W, 1)
	2	(W, 2)
	3	(W, 3)
	4	(W, 4)
	5	(W, 5)
	6	(W, 6)

B represents black
W represents white

2.

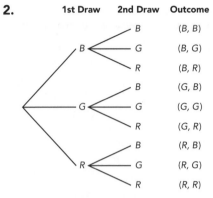

1st Draw	2nd Draw	Outcome
B	B	(B, B)
	G	(B, G)
	R	(B, R)
G	B	(G, B)
	G	(G, G)
	R	(G, R)
R	B	(R, B)
	G	(R, G)
	R	(R, R)

B represents black
G represents green
R represents red

3.

Bead	Coin	Outcome
G	H	(G, H)
	T	(G, T)
R	H	(R, H)
	T	(R, T)
W	H	(W, H)
	T	(W, T)
B	H	(B, H)
	T	(B, T)

G represents green
W represents white
R represents red
B represents black

4.

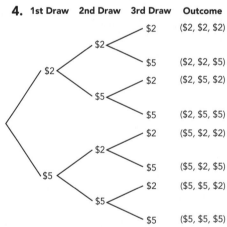

1st Draw	2nd Draw	3rd Draw	Outcome
$2	$2	$2	($2, $2, $2)
		$5	($2, $2, $5)
	$5	$2	($2, $5, $2)
		$5	($2, $5, $5)
$5	$2	$2	($5, $2, $2)
		$5	($5, $2, $5)
	$5	$2	($5, $5, $2)
		$5	($5, $5, $5)

5.

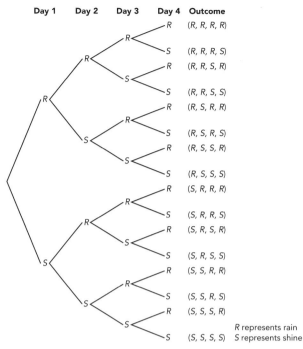

Day 1	Day 2	Day 3	Day 4	Outcome

(R, R, R, R)
(R, R, R, S)
(R, R, S, R)
(R, R, S, S)
(R, S, R, R)
(R, S, R, S)
(R, S, S, R)
(R, S, S, S)
(S, R, R, R)
(S, R, R, S)
(S, R, S, R)
(S, R, S, S)
(S, S, R, R)
(S, S, R, S)
(S, S, S, R)
(S, S, S, S)

R represents rain
S represents shine

6.

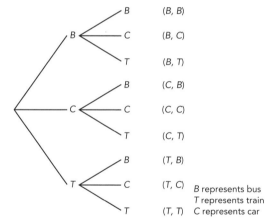

Saturday	Sunday	Outcome

(B, B)
(B, C)
(B, T)
(C, B)
(C, C)
(C, T)
(T, B)
(T, C)
(T, T)

B represents bus
T represents train
C represents car

7. a)

Coin	Die	Outcome

H1
H2
H3
H4
(H5)
(H6)
T1
T2
T3
T4
T5
T6

H represents heads
T represents tails

b) Total number of possible outcomes = 12
The number of winning outcomes is 2.

P(winning the game in one try) $= \dfrac{2}{12}$

$\qquad\qquad\qquad\qquad\qquad\quad = \dfrac{1}{6}$

c) P(losing the game in one try)
$= 1 - $ P(winning the game in one try)
$= 1 - \dfrac{1}{6}$
$= \dfrac{5}{6}$

8. a)

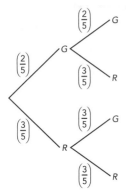

1st Party Hat   2nd Party Hat   Outcome

$\left(\frac{2}{5}\right)$ G   (G, G)

$\left(\frac{2}{5}\right)$ G

$\left(\frac{3}{5}\right)$ R   (G, R)

$\left(\frac{3}{5}\right)$ G   (R, G)

$\left(\frac{3}{5}\right)$ R

$\left(\frac{3}{5}\right)$ R   (R, R)

G represents green
R represents red

b) $P(R, R) = P(R) \cdot P(R)$

$= \frac{3}{5} \cdot \frac{3}{5}$

$= \frac{9}{25}$

c) $P(G, R) = P(G) \cdot P(R)$

$= \frac{2}{5} \cdot \frac{3}{5}$

$= \frac{6}{25}$

b) $P(R, R) = P(R) \cdot P(R)$

$= \frac{2}{6} \cdot \frac{2}{6}$

$= \frac{4}{36}$

$= \frac{1}{9}$

c) $P(Y, Y) = P(Y) \cdot P(Y)$

$= \frac{3}{6} \cdot \frac{3}{6}$

$= \frac{9}{36}$

$= \frac{1}{4}$

d) $P(G, G) = P(G) \cdot P(G)$

$= \frac{1}{6} \cdot \frac{1}{6}$

$= \frac{1}{36}$

P(different colors)
= 1 − P(same colors)
= 1 − [P(R, R) + P(Y, Y) + P(G, G)]
$= 1 - \left(\frac{1}{9} + \frac{1}{4} + \frac{1}{36}\right)$
$= 1 - \frac{14}{36}$
$= \frac{11}{18}$

9. a)

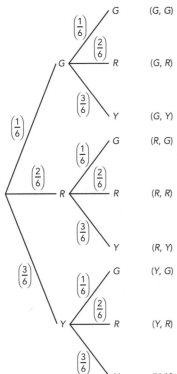

1st Selection   2nd Selection   Outcome

$\left(\frac{1}{6}\right)$ G   (G, G)

G $\left(\frac{2}{6}\right)$ R   (G, R)

$\left(\frac{3}{6}\right)$ Y   (G, Y)

$\left(\frac{1}{6}\right)$ G   (R, G)

$\left(\frac{2}{6}\right)$ R $\left(\frac{2}{6}\right)$ R   (R, R)

$\left(\frac{3}{6}\right)$ Y   (R, Y)

$\left(\frac{1}{6}\right)$ G   (Y, G)

$\left(\frac{3}{6}\right)$ Y $\left(\frac{2}{6}\right)$ R   (Y, R)

$\left(\frac{3}{6}\right)$ Y   (Y, Y)

$\left(\frac{1}{6}\right)$

G represents green
R represents red
Y represents yellow

10. a)

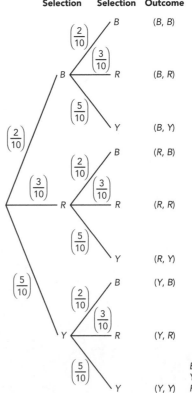

1st Selection   2nd Selection   Outcome

$\left(\frac{2}{10}\right)$ B   (B, B)

B $\left(\frac{3}{10}\right)$ R   (B, R)

$\left(\frac{5}{10}\right)$ Y   (B, Y)

$\left(\frac{2}{10}\right)$ B   (R, B)

$\left(\frac{3}{10}\right)$ R $\left(\frac{3}{10}\right)$ R   (R, R)

$\left(\frac{5}{10}\right)$ Y   (R, Y)

$\left(\frac{2}{10}\right)$ B   (Y, B)

$\left(\frac{5}{10}\right)$ Y $\left(\frac{3}{10}\right)$ R   (Y, R)

$\left(\frac{2}{10}\right)$

$\left(\frac{5}{10}\right)$ Y   (Y, Y)

B represents blue
Y represents yellow
R represents red

b) $P(R, R) = P(R) \cdot P(R)$

$$= \frac{3}{10} \cdot \frac{3}{10}$$

$$= \frac{9}{100}$$

c) $P(B, Y) = P(B) \cdot P(Y)$

$$= \frac{2}{10} \cdot \frac{5}{10}$$

$$= \frac{10}{100}$$

$$= \frac{1}{10}$$

d) $P(Y, R) = P(Y) \cdot P(R)$

$$= \frac{5}{10} \cdot \frac{3}{10}$$

$$= \frac{15}{100}$$

$$= \frac{3}{20}$$

11. a) $P(\text{odd number on red die}) = \frac{3}{6}$

$$= \frac{1}{2}$$

$P(\text{odd number on white die}) = \frac{3}{6}$

$$= \frac{1}{2}$$

$P(\text{odd number on both dice}) = \frac{1}{2} \cdot \frac{1}{2}$

$$= \frac{1}{4}$$

b) $P(\text{even number on white die}) = \frac{3}{6}$

$$= \frac{1}{2}$$

$P(\text{odd number on red die, even number on white die})$

$= P(\text{odd number on red die}) \cdot P(\text{even number on white die})$

$$= \frac{1}{2} \cdot \frac{1}{2}$$

$$= \frac{1}{4}$$

c) $P(\text{number greater than 4 on red die})$

$$= \frac{2}{6}$$

$$= \frac{1}{3}$$

$P(\text{number greater than 4 on white die})$

$$= \frac{2}{6}$$

$$= \frac{1}{3}$$

$P(\text{number greater than 4 on both dice})$

$$= \frac{1}{3} \cdot \frac{1}{3}$$

$$= \frac{1}{9}$$

12. $P(\text{late at least one of any 2 days})$
$= 1 - P(\text{on time for both days})$
$= 1 - P(\text{on time for 1st day}) \cdot P(\text{on time for 2nd day})$

$$= 1 - \frac{9}{10} \cdot \frac{9}{10}$$

$$= 1 - \frac{81}{100}$$

$$= \frac{19}{100}$$

13. On any spin,

$$P(G) = \frac{60}{360}$$

$$= \frac{1}{6}$$

$$P(B) = \frac{120}{360}$$

$$= \frac{1}{3}$$

$$P(R) = \frac{180}{360}$$

$$= \frac{1}{2}$$

a) $P(\text{same color on both spins})$
$= P(G, G) + P(B, B) + P(R, R)$

$$= \left(\frac{1}{6} \cdot \frac{1}{6}\right) + \left(\frac{1}{3} \cdot \frac{1}{3}\right) + \left(\frac{1}{2} \cdot \frac{1}{2}\right)$$

$$= \frac{1}{36} + \frac{1}{9} + \frac{1}{4}$$

$$= \frac{7}{18}$$

b) Let B' be the event that the indicator does not point to the blue sector.

$$P(B') = 1 - P(B)$$

$$= 1 - \frac{1}{3}$$

$$= \frac{2}{3}$$

$P(\text{blue at least once})$
$= 1 - P(B' \text{ on the 1st spin}) \cdot P(B' \text{ on the 2nd spin})$

$$= 1 - \frac{2}{3} \cdot \frac{2}{3}$$

$$= 1 - \frac{4}{9}$$

$$= \frac{5}{9}$$

P(number greater than 4 on both dice)

$$= \frac{1}{3} \cdot \frac{1}{3}$$

$$= \frac{1}{9}$$

14. $P(1 \text{ or } 2) = \dfrac{2}{6}$

$\qquad\qquad = \dfrac{1}{3}$

$\quad P(3 \text{ or } 4) = \dfrac{2}{6}$

$\qquad\qquad = \dfrac{1}{3}$

$\quad P(5 \text{ or } 6) = \dfrac{2}{6}$

$\qquad\qquad = \dfrac{1}{3}$

a) To win after tossing the die once, the number tossed must be 5 or 6.
P(win after one toss) = P(5 or 6)

$\qquad\qquad\qquad = \dfrac{1}{3}$

b) To win after two tosses:

Either 1 or 2 on the 1st toss, followed by 5 or 6 on the 2nd toss, or 3 or 4 on the 1st toss, followed by 3 or 4 on the 2nd toss, or 3 or 4 on the 1st toss, followed by 5 or 6 on the 2nd toss

P(win after 2 tosses)

= P(1 or 2) · P(5 or 6) + P(3 or 4) · P(3 or 4) + P(3 or 4) · P(5 or 6)

$= \left(\dfrac{1}{3}\cdot\dfrac{1}{3}\right)+\left(\dfrac{1}{3}\cdot\dfrac{1}{3}\right)+\left(\dfrac{1}{3}\cdot\dfrac{1}{3}\right)$

$= \dfrac{1}{3}$

15. No. The probability of a coin landing in the shaded part depends on the areas of the shaded and unshaded parts.

Area of the shaded part = $\pi(3)^2$

$\qquad\qquad\qquad\quad = 9\pi \text{ in}^2$

Area of the whole target = $\pi(6)^2$

$\qquad\qquad\qquad\quad = 36\pi \text{ in}^2$

So, P(landing in shaded part)

$= \dfrac{\text{Area of the shaded part}}{\text{Area of target}}$

$= \dfrac{9\pi}{36\pi}$

$= \dfrac{1}{4}$

Lesson 11.4

1. Dependent

2. Independent

3. Dependent

4. Independent

5.

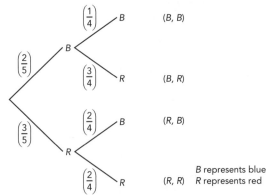

6.

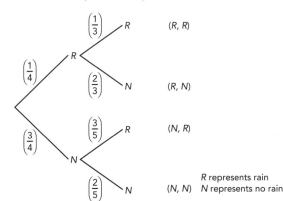

7.

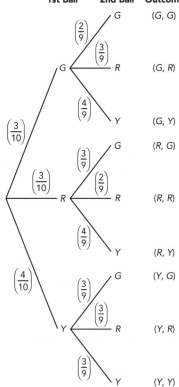

a) P(2 red balls)
= P(R, R)
= P(R) · P(R after R)
$$= \frac{3}{10} \cdot \frac{2}{9}$$
$$= \frac{6}{90}$$
$$= \frac{1}{15}$$

The probability of drawing two red balls is $\frac{1}{15}$.

b) P(at least 1 yellow ball)
= P(G, Y) + P(R, Y) + P(Y, G) + P(Y, R) + P(Y, Y)
= P(G) · P(Y after G) + P(R) · P(Y after R) + P(Y) · P(G after Y) + P(Y) · P(R after Y) + P(Y) · P(Y after Y)
$$= \frac{3}{10} \cdot \frac{4}{9} \cdot \frac{3}{10} \cdot \frac{4}{9} \cdot \frac{4}{10} \cdot \frac{3}{9} \cdot \frac{4}{10} \cdot \frac{3}{9} \cdot \frac{4}{10} \cdot \frac{3}{9}$$
$$= \frac{12}{90} + \frac{12}{90} + \frac{12}{90} + \frac{12}{90} + \frac{12}{90}$$
$$= \frac{60}{90}$$
$$= \frac{2}{3}$$

The probability of drawing at least one yellow ball is $\frac{2}{3}$.

8.

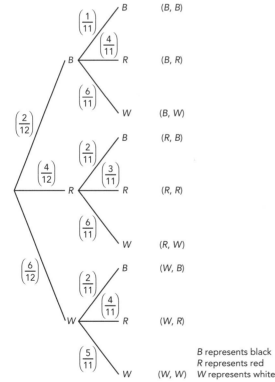

1st Sock   2nd Sock   Outcome

B represents black
R represents red
W represents white

a) P(same color socks)
= P(B, B) + P(R, R) + P(W, W)
= P(B) · P(B after B) + P(R) · P(R after R) + P(W) · P(W after W)
$$= \frac{2}{12} \cdot \frac{1}{11} + \frac{4}{12} \cdot \frac{3}{11} + \frac{6}{12} \cdot \frac{5}{11}$$
$$= \frac{2}{132} + \frac{12}{132} + \frac{30}{132}$$
$$= \frac{44}{132}$$
$$= \frac{1}{3}$$

The probability of picking socks of the same color is $\frac{1}{3}$.

b) P(different color socks)
= 1 − P(same color socks)
$$= 1 - \frac{1}{3}$$
$$= \frac{2}{3}$$

The probability of picking socks of different colors is $\frac{1}{3}$.

9.

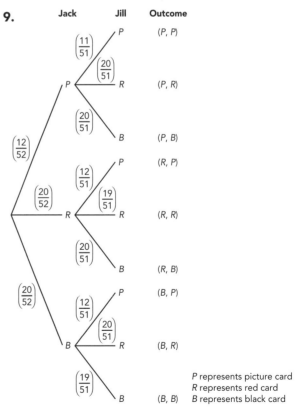

Jack   Jill   Outcome

P represents picture card
R represents red card
B represents black card

a) P(both picture cards)

$= P(P, P)$

$= P(P) \cdot P(P \text{ after } P)$

$= \dfrac{12}{52} \cdot \dfrac{11}{51}$

$= \dfrac{132}{2{,}652}$

$= \dfrac{11}{221}$

The probability of Jack and Jill both picking picture cards is $\dfrac{11}{121}$.

b) P(one red card, one black card)

$= P(R, B) + P(B, R)$

$= P(R) \cdot P(B \text{ after } R) + P(B) \cdot P(R \text{ after } B)$

$= \dfrac{20}{52} \cdot \dfrac{20}{51} + \dfrac{20}{52} \cdot \dfrac{20}{51}$

$= \dfrac{400}{2{,}652} + \dfrac{400}{2{,}652}$

$= \dfrac{800}{2{,}652}$

$= \dfrac{200}{663}$

The probability of Jack picking a red card and Jill picking a black card, or vice versa, is $\dfrac{200}{663}$.

10. a) $x = \dfrac{1}{3}, y = 1 - \dfrac{1}{3} = \dfrac{2}{3}$

$z = 1 - \dfrac{1}{4} = \dfrac{3}{4}$

P(rains exactly one day)

$= P(R, N) + P(N, R)$

$= P(R) \cdot P(N \text{ after } R) +$
$\quad P(N) \cdot P(R \text{ after } N)$

$= \dfrac{1}{3} \cdot \dfrac{3}{5} + \dfrac{2}{3} \cdot \dfrac{1}{4}$

$= \dfrac{3}{15} + \dfrac{2}{12}$

$= \dfrac{12}{60} + \dfrac{10}{60}$

$= \dfrac{22}{60}$

$= \dfrac{11}{30}$

b) P(rains both days) $= \dfrac{3}{10}$

$\qquad\qquad\qquad\quad = P(R, R)$

$P(R) \cdot P(R \text{ after } R) = \dfrac{3}{10}$

$x \cdot \dfrac{2}{5} = \dfrac{3}{10}$

$x \cdot \dfrac{2}{5} \cdot \dfrac{5}{2} = \dfrac{3}{10} \cdot \dfrac{5}{2}$

$x = \dfrac{15}{20}$

$x = \dfrac{3}{4}$

$y = 1 - x$

$= 1 - \dfrac{3}{4}$

$= \dfrac{1}{4}$

So, $x = \dfrac{3}{4}$ and $y = \dfrac{1}{4}$.

11. a)

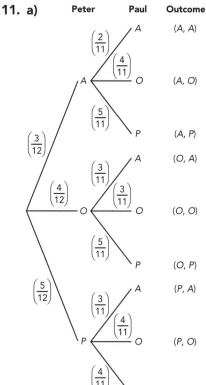

A represents apple
O represents orange
P represents pear

b) P(Peter selects apple, Paul selects pear)

$= P(A, P)$

$= P(A) \cdot P(P \text{ after } A)$

$= \dfrac{3}{12} \cdot \dfrac{5}{11}$

$= \dfrac{15}{132}$

$= \dfrac{5}{44}$

The probability of Peter selecting an apple and Paul selecting a pear is $\dfrac{5}{44}$.

c) P(Peter and Paul select same type of fruit)

$= P(A, A) + P(O, O) + P(P, P)$

$= P(A) \cdot P(A \text{ after } A) + P(O)$
$\cdot P(O \text{ after } O) + P(P) \cdot P(P \text{ after } P)$

$= \dfrac{3}{12} \cdot \dfrac{2}{11} + \dfrac{4}{12} \cdot \dfrac{3}{11} + \dfrac{5}{12} \cdot \dfrac{4}{11}$

$= \dfrac{6}{132} + \dfrac{12}{132} + \dfrac{20}{132}$

$= \dfrac{38}{132}$

$= \dfrac{19}{66}$

The probability of Peter and Paul both selecting the same type of fruit is $\dfrac{19}{66}$.

d) P(Peter or Paul selects an orange)

$= P(A, O) + P(O, A) + P(O, P) + P(P, O)$

$= P(A) \cdot P(O \text{ after } A) + P(O) \cdot P(A \text{ after } O)$
$+ P(O) \cdot P(P \text{ after } O) + P(P)$
$\cdot P(O \text{ after } P)$

$= \dfrac{3}{12} \cdot \dfrac{4}{11} + \dfrac{4}{12} \cdot \dfrac{3}{11} + \dfrac{4}{12} \cdot \dfrac{5}{11} + \dfrac{5}{12} \cdot \dfrac{4}{11}$

$= \dfrac{12}{132} + \dfrac{12}{132} + \dfrac{20}{132} + \dfrac{20}{132}$

$= \dfrac{64}{132}$

$= \dfrac{16}{33}$

The probability that either Peter or Paul selects an orange is $\dfrac{16}{33}$.

12. a)

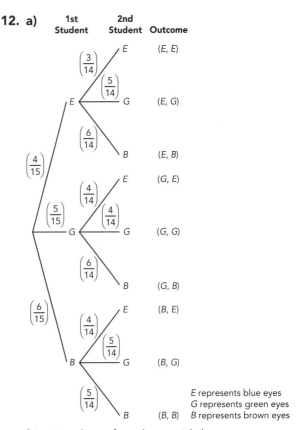

E represents blue eyes
G represents green eyes
B represents brown eyes

b) Number of students with brown eyes

$= 15 - 4 - 5$

$= 6$

P(first student has brown eyes)

$= \dfrac{6}{15}$

The probability that the first student called has brown eyes is $\dfrac{6}{15}$.

c) P(first student blue eyes, second student green eyes)

$= P(E, G)$

$= P(E) \cdot P(G \text{ after } E)$

$= \dfrac{4}{15} \cdot \dfrac{5}{14}$

$= \dfrac{20}{210}$

$= \dfrac{2}{21}$

The probability that the first student called has blue eyes, and the second student called has green eyes is $\dfrac{2}{21}$.

d) P(both students have eyes of same color)

$= P(E, E) + P(G, G) + P(N, N)$

$= P(E) \cdot P(E \text{ after } E) + P(G) \cdot P(G \text{ after } G) + P(N) \cdot P(N \text{ after } N)$

$= \dfrac{4}{15} \cdot \dfrac{3}{14} + \dfrac{5}{15} \cdot \dfrac{4}{14} + \dfrac{6}{15} \cdot \dfrac{5}{14}$

$= \dfrac{12}{210} + \dfrac{20}{210} + \dfrac{30}{210}$

$= \dfrac{62}{210}$

$= \dfrac{31}{105}$

The probability that both students called have eyes of the same color is $\dfrac{31}{105}$.

13. a) P(Mary eats almond) $= \dfrac{1}{3}$

$\dfrac{x}{12} = \dfrac{1}{3}$

$\dfrac{x}{12} \cdot 12 = \dfrac{1}{3} \cdot 12$

$x = 4$

b)

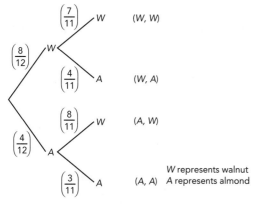

Mary · Nancy · Outcome

$\left(\dfrac{7}{11}\right)$ W (W, W)

$\left(\dfrac{8}{12}\right)$ W

$\left(\dfrac{4}{11}\right)$ A (W, A)

$\left(\dfrac{8}{11}\right)$ W (A, W)

$\left(\dfrac{4}{12}\right)$ A

$\left(\dfrac{3}{11}\right)$ A (A, A)

W represents walnut
A represents almond

c) P(eat same type of nut)

$= P(W, W) + P(A, A)$

$= P(W) \cdot P(W \text{ after } W) + P(A) \cdot P(A \text{ after } A)$

$= \dfrac{8}{12} \cdot \dfrac{7}{11} + \dfrac{4}{12} \cdot \dfrac{3}{11}$

$= \dfrac{56}{132} + \dfrac{12}{132}$

$= \dfrac{68}{132}$

$= \dfrac{17}{33}$

The probability that both Mary and Nancy eat the same type of nut is $\dfrac{17}{33}$.

14. a) P(Alan wins both games)

$= P(\text{Alan wins 1st game}) \cdot P(\text{Alan wins 2nd game after winning 1st game})$

$= 0.6 \cdot x$

$0.6x = 0.42$

$\dfrac{0.6x}{0.6} = \dfrac{0.42}{0.6}$

$x = 0.7$

b)

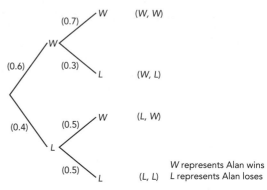

1st Game · 2nd Game · Outcome

(0.7) W (W, W)

(0.6) W

(0.3) L (W, L)

(0.4) L

(0.5) W (L, W)

(0.5) L (L, L)

W represents Alan wins
L represents Alan loses

c) P(Bob wins both games)

$= P(\text{Alan loses both games})$

$= P(L, L)$

$= P(L) \cdot P(L \text{ after } L)$

$= 0.4 \cdot 0.5$

$= 0.2$

The probability that Bob wins both games is 0.2.

d) P(Bob wins at least one game)

$= P(\text{Alan loses at least one game})$

$= P(W, L) + P(L, W) + P(L, L)$

$= P(W) \cdot P(L \text{ after } W) + P(L) \cdot P(W \text{ after } L) + P(L) \cdot P(L \text{ after } L)$

$= 0.6 \cdot 0.3 + 0.4 \cdot 0.5 + 0.4 \cdot 0.5$

$= 0.18 + 0.2 + 0.2$

$= 0.58$

The probability that Bob wins at least one game is 0.58.

Brain @ Work

1. When Dominic is serving, he will get points if his first serve is not a fault, or his first serve is a fault but the second serve is not a fault.

Percent of points obtained if the first serve is not a fault

$$= \frac{1}{4} \cdot 75\%$$

$$= 18.75\%$$

Percent of points obtained in the second serve

$$= \frac{3}{4} \cdot \frac{3}{5} \cdot 55\%$$

$$= 24.75\%$$

Total percent of points won if Dominic is serving

$$= 18.75\% + 24.75\%$$

$$= 43.5\%$$

2. a) Largest perfect square

$$= \sqrt{100,000} = 1,000$$

The perfect squares from 1 to 1,000,000 are $1^2, 2^2, 3^2,..., 1,000^2$

Number of perfect squares $= 1,000$

Probability of choosing a perfect square

$$= \frac{1,000}{1,000,000} = \frac{1}{1,000}$$

Probability of choosing a nonperfect square

$$= 1 - \frac{1}{1,000} = \frac{999}{1,000}$$

b) Approximate number of primes

$$= \frac{7.24}{100} \cdot 1,000,000$$

$$= 72,400$$

Cumulative Practice for Chapters 10 and 11

1.

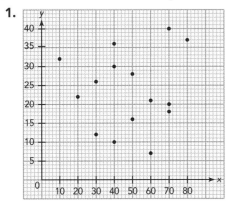

There are no outliers.

2.

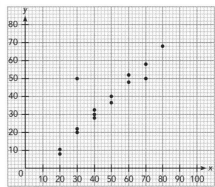

The data point (30, 50) is an outlier.

3. Strong, positive, linear association

4. Strong, negative, linear association

5. Line A

6.

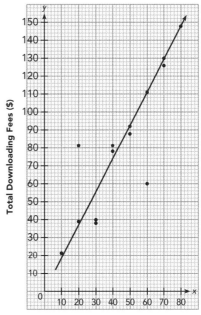

Downloading Fees for Songs

7.

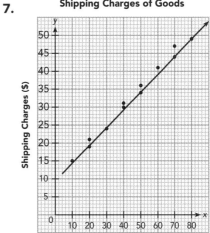

Shipping Charges of Goods

8. Qualitative

9. Quantitative

10. a) Number of males who prefer guided tours
= Total number of males −
Number of males who
prefer self-guided tours
= 11 − 8
= 3
3 males prefer guided tours.

b) Number of females who prefer
self-guided tours
= Total number of females −
Number of females who
prefer guided tours
= 9 − 5
= 4
4 females prefer self-guided tours.

c) Total number of students who prefer
guided tours
= 3 + 5
= 8

d) Total number of students who prefer
self-guided tours
= 8 + 4
= 12

Tour Preference

		Guided	Self-Guided	Total
Gender	**Male**	3	8	11
	Female	5	4	9
	Total	8	12	20

11.

Cycle

		Yes	No	Total
Walk	**Yes**	5	10	15
	No	4	1	5
	Total	9	11	20

12. Simple event

13. This is a compound event. There are two
simple events: drawing the first A-tile and
drawing the second A-tile.

14.

Spinner B

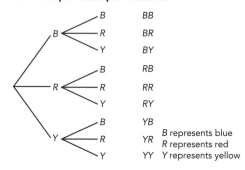

Spinner A	1	2	3	4	5
1	(1, 1)	(2, 1)	(3, 1)	(4, 1)	(5, 1)
2	(1, 2)	(2, 2)	(3, 2)	(4, 2)	(5, 2)
3	(1, 3)	(2, 3)	(3, 3)	(4, 3)	(5, 3)

There are 15 possible outcomes.

15. a)

1st Spin	2nd Spin	Outcome
B	B	BB
	R	BR
	Y	BY
R	B	RB
	R	RR
	Y	RY
Y	B	YB
	R	YR
	Y	YY

B represents blue
R represents red
Y represents yellow

b) There are 9 possible outcomes.

16. a) and **b)**

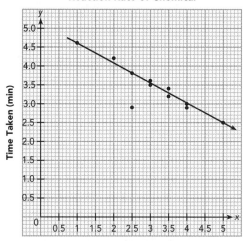

Reaction Rate of Chemical

The data point (2.5, 2.9) is an outlier.

c) The line of best fit passes through the points (1, 4.6) and (5, 2.5).

$$m = \frac{2.5 - 4.6}{5 - 1} = \frac{-2.1}{4} = -0.525$$

Using the equation in slope-intercept form,

$$y = mx + b$$
$$4.6 = -0.525(1) + b$$
$$4.6 = -0.525 + b$$
$$4.6 + 0.525 = -0.525 + b + 0.525$$
$$b = 5.125$$
$$y = -0.525x + 5.125$$

The equation of the line of best fit is $y = -0.525x + 5.125$.

17. a) and **b)**

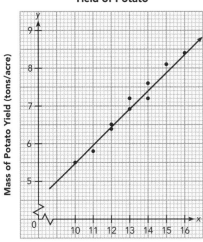

Yield of Potato

Mass of Potato Yield (tons/acre) — y-axis

Amount of Rainfall (in.) — x-axis

b) The line of best fit passes through the points (10, 5.5) and (16, 8.4).

$$m = \frac{8.4 - 5.5}{16 - 10} = \frac{2.9}{6} \approx 0.48$$

Using the equation in slope-intercept form,

$$y = mx + b$$
$$5.5 = 0.48(10) + b$$
$$5.5 = 4.8 + b$$
$$5.5 - 4.8 = 4.8 + b - 4.8$$
$$b = 0.7$$
$$y = 0.48x + 0.7$$

The equation of the line of best fit is $y = 0.48x + 0.7$.

c) Using the equation $y = 0.48x + 0.7$, substitute $14\frac{1}{2}$ for x.

$$y = 0.48 \cdot 14\frac{1}{2} + 0.7 = 7.66$$

An annual yield of about 8 tons/acre could be expected when the annual rainfall is $14\frac{1}{2}$ inches.

18. a)

Ball (Bag A)	Cube (Bag B)		
	Blue (B)	**Red (R)**	**Yellow (Y)**
Red (R)	BR	RR	YR
Yellow (Y)	BY	RY	YY

b) P(ball and cube are of the same color)

$$= \frac{1}{6} + \frac{1}{6}$$
$$= \frac{1}{3}$$

19. a)

Spinner	Die					
	1	**2**	**3**	**4**	**5**	**6**
1	(1, 1)	(2, 1)	(3, 1)	(4, 1)	(5, 1)	(6, 1)
2	(1, 2)	(2, 2)	(3, 2)	(4, 2)	(5, 2)	(6, 2)
3	(1, 3)	(2, 3)	(3, 3)	(4, 3)	(5, 3)	(6, 3)

b) P(number from spinner ≥ number from die) $= \frac{6}{18}$

$$= \frac{1}{3}$$

20. a)

Spinner	Ball				
+	**1**	**2**	**3**	**4**	**5**
1	2	3	4	5	6
2	3	4	5	6	7
3	4	5	6	7	8
4	5	6	7	8	9

b) There are 20 possible outcomes. Number of outcomes with a sum greater than 6 is 6.

$$P(\text{sum} > 6) = \frac{6}{20} = \frac{3}{10}$$

21. a)

1st Die	2nd Die					
−	**1**	**2**	**3**	**4**	**5**	**6**
1	0	1	2	3	4	5
2	1	0	1	2	3	4
3	2	1	0	1	2	3
4	3	2	1	0	1	2
5	4	3	2	1	0	1
6	5	4	3	2	1	0

b) There are 36 possible outcomes. There are 16 possible outcomes with the absolute value of the difference being less than 2.

$$P(\text{difference} < 2) = \frac{16}{36} = \frac{4}{9}$$

22. a)

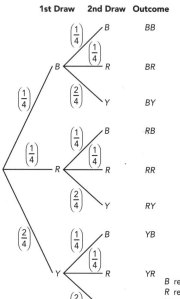

1st Draw   2nd Draw   Outcome

B represents blue
R represents red
Y represents yellow

b) P(both red or both yellow)
$$= P(RR) + P(YY)$$
$$= \frac{1}{4} \cdot \frac{1}{4} + \frac{2}{4} \cdot \frac{2}{4}$$
$$= \frac{5}{16}$$

23. a)

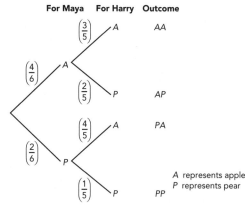

For Maya   For Harry   Outcome

A represents apple
P represents pear

b) P (different fruits)
$$= P(AP) + P(PA)$$
$$= \frac{4}{6} \cdot \frac{2}{5} + \frac{2}{6} \cdot \frac{4}{5}$$
$$= \frac{8}{15}$$

24. a) Number of boys who support Team $C = 25 - 7 - 8 = 10$

$$P(\text{boy supports Team C}) = \frac{10}{25} = \frac{2}{5}$$

b)

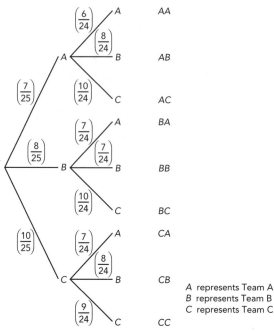

1st Boy   2nd Boy   Outcome

A represents Team A
B represents Team B
C represents Team C

P(both boys support Team A or both boys support Team B)
$$= P(AA) + P(BB)$$
$$= \frac{7}{25} \cdot \frac{6}{24} + \frac{8}{25} \cdot \frac{7}{24}$$
$$= \frac{47}{300}$$

25. a) Area of $\triangle MAN = \frac{1}{8}$ area of square $ABCD$

Area of region in the square but outside $\triangle MAN = \frac{7}{8}$ area of square

$$P(\text{point not inside } \triangle MAN) = \frac{7}{8}$$

b)

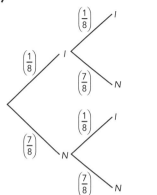

1st Point   2nd Point   Outcome

II

IN

NI

NN

I represents a point
inside △*MAN*
N represents a point
outside △*MAN*

P(1 point inside △*MAN* and the other is
not)

$$= P(IN) + P(NI)$$

$$= \frac{1}{8} \cdot \frac{7}{8} + \frac{7}{8} \cdot \frac{1}{8}$$

$$= \frac{7}{32}$$

26. a)   P(boy) = $\frac{5}{9}$

b)   After a boy has been chosen first, the
remainder are 4 boys and 4 girls.

P(boy) = $\frac{4}{8} = \frac{1}{2}$

27. a)

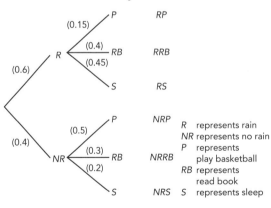

Weather   Activity   Outcome

(0.6)

R

(0.15)   P   RP

(0.4) RB   RRB

(0.45)   S   RS

(0.4)

NR

(0.5)   P   NRP

(0.3) RB   NRRB

(0.2)   S   NRS

R   represents rain
NR represents no rain
P   represents
    play basketball
RB represents
    read book
S   represents sleep

b)   P(Susan reads a book)
= P(*RRB*) + P(*NRRB*)
= 0.6 · 0.4 + 0.4 · 0.3
= 0.36

c)   P(does not rain and Susan goes to sleep)
= P(*NRS*)
= 0.4 · 0.2
= 0.08

d)   P(Susan plays basketball)
= P(*RP*) + P(*NRP*)
= 0.6 · 0.15 + 0.4 · 0.5
= 0.29

28. a)

	Male	Female	Total
Pink	0	2	2
Blue	3	1	4
Black	2	1	3
Green	2	1	3
Total	7	5	12

b)   No male prefers pink. Most males prefer
blue.

BLANK

BLANK

BLANK